PRAISE FOR CANCERING

"Lauren Huffmaster has created a beautiful healing guide for anyone thrust into the world of cancer. From the first page, she grabs your hand and leads you forward through self-exploration, helping to turn chaos into peace by reminding you that you are not alone and there are proven strategies that you can implement to not only persevere, but to thrive. Spiritual and mental health are often overlooked or deprioritized after a cancer diagnosis, but in over twenty years of working in cancer patient advocacy, I have seen firsthand dramatically better outcomes when both the physical and emotional needs of patients have been simultaneously embraced."
-Kristin Holman Olson, Oncology Patient Advocate

"This book is truly inspirational and has touched my soul. Thank you for bringing attention to the emotional side effects of cancer that impact all patients and their families. Your book made me feel connected to a community which shared my emotional pain and struggles. I want each member of my family to read this beautiful and long-overdue work of art. I love your gentle reminder that we are not defined by this disease, just strengthened by it. Turning "Pain into Purpose" is my new life's motto. Your book is a beautiful reminder that serving others creates a sense of strength and belonging. The sense of isolation is real, and your words brought me a sense of connection and true understanding of what one goes through during this journey."
-Petie Huether, Cancer Survivor

PRAISE FOR CANCERING

"*Cancering* is an inspirational exploration of the oft-ignored emotional impacts of cancer—for those diagnosed or who are supporting a friend or loved one with the disease. The book is filled with insights and practical approaches to shine a light on this unmet need, change fear to joy, and help us all reframe our view of what's possible living with, through, and beyond cancer."
-*Stu Dorman, Vice President, Oncology Business Unit Head at Gilead Sciences*

"Reading *Cancering* is one of the most impactful steps I have taken in my own cancer journey as it left me with a new motivation to thrive rather than merely survive. The term "cancering" gives hope to a word that is commonly used to describe something evil or malignant that spreads destructively. There were so many pivotal take-aways that I found myself taking notes in a journal to help me refocus my energy to own my power and potential. Lauren writes with a level of vulnerability that is empowering and helped put into words some of the emotions and challenges I have experienced myself but didn't have a language to express. The themes of hope and irrational optimism communicated through vivid metaphors and symbolism are firmly supported with a balance of research, defining terminology, experience, and transparency. There are even reflections supporting you to take concrete action. Lauren's statement "fear is more detrimental to legacy than cancer" has been on my heart daily since reading it. I have been applying her content about fear to make hope and horizon vision a conscious choice. Cancering should be required reading for everyone crossing the cancer path: patients, caregivers, physicians, social workers, and nurses."
-*Melanie Anderson, Cancer Patient*

CANCERING

Exploring the Seasons of Emotional Healing

By Lauren Huffmaster

Adventure Therapy Foundation Publishing

CANCERING
First edition: June, 2024
© 2024, Lauren Huffmaster
© 2024, Adventure Therapy Foundation Publishing
Oakley, California

Printed in United States of America
ISBN: 9798322614210
Imprint: Independently Published
Printed by KDP Publishing
Edited by Angela Warner
Design by Guerra Graphics

Dedication

*To the co-survivors in my life,
my beloved husband, and three beautiful
girls. Thank you for choosing to walk
with me in faith, hope, and love.*

Contents

xv   **PREFACE**

Introduction

1   I Am Lauren
        The Dream of What Can Be
        Purpose

Part 1
17   The Emotional Side Effects of Cancer

20   **CHAPTER 1: FEAR**
        Irrational Optimism
        Joy and Identity
        Fear and Uncertainty
        Take Action

36   **CHAPTER 2: ISOLATION**
      Isolation and Identity
      Isolation and Belonging
      Isolation as a Season
      Strength and Weakness
      Take Action

50   **CHAPTER 3: IDENTITY**
      Protecting Yourself from Identity Theft
      Stages of Life
      Mourning a Broken Identity
      Values vs. Expectations
      Take Every Thought Captive
      Take Action

72   **PART 1 CONCLUSION:**
      A TYPICAL EMOTIONAL RESPONSE TO CANCER

Part 2
79   The Healing Process

87   **CHAPTER 4: FIRE**
      The Diagnosis
      Strength
      Take Action

99 CHAPTER 5: VOID
Beginning Again
Gifts
Two Types of Dreams: Calling and Casting
Following a Dream
Take Action

113 CHAPTER 6: GROWTH
Witnessing Growth
Uncovering Our Roots
Self-Discovery
Hope That Fuels Growth
Growing Hope
Urgency of the Day
Pruning Pain
Take Action

130 CHAPTER 7: RESTORATION
Restoration of Others
Restoring Expectations
Take Action

140 CHAPTER 8: GIVING
Shaping Ourselves for the Good of Others
Giving by Receiving
What Giving Means to Others
Giving Hope
What Giving Means to You
Take Action

150 PART 2 CONCLUSION:
MILESTONES FOR EMOTIONAL GROWTH

Part 3
155 Cancering

157 CHAPTER 9: EMOTIONAL HEALTH
MOVING FORWARD
Rest
Water
Healthy Food
Movement
Stepping Forward
Take Action

170 PART 3 CONCLUSION:
THE 30,000-FOOT VIEW

174 EPILOGUE

PREFACE

I was diagnosed with terminal cancer as a young adult. This is what most people know about me. Like millions of other cancer survivors, I dealt with crippling fear, anxiety attacks, sleepless nights, broken expectations, and constant wrestling with my mortality. I never went to counseling, and none of my eight oncology teams ever offered me a counseling referral.

I never found another survivor to look up to or turn to for support. I met a few women I thought would partner with me along the road, but each died, as terminal patients often do. Each time, I was left alone with my thoughts and desire to turn this cancer experience into something more.

My preferred tool for processing the emotional burdens of cancer was to escape into nature. My family and I went on countless weekend retreats. These escapes allowed me the mental space to see beyond the doctors' offices and the emotional walls I felt restricted by. Finding a new perspective was easy for me when I was among the trees.

After two years of treatment, I realized cancer had defined a significant portion of my young girls' lives. I did not want them to look into their future and only see hardship.

I wanted to teach my girls that life will have difficult seasons, but it will also have seasons of joy. To embrace the best version of childlike joy possible, we purchased a season pass to Disneyland. We spent a year celebrating in Disneyland because every great pull downward needs an equal and opposite upward moment. While silent retreats into nature reset my mind, my family needed to find restoration through spontaneous fun and better-than-expected moments.

Since the early days of cancer, my dominant source of strength has been my spiritual life. I am a Christian and believe what we know about Jesus is true. My faith allows me to attach myself to hundreds of impossible situations that others have faced throughout history. With nothing but faith in a God who loves them, they not only overcame their circumstance but also inspired generations. These stories renew my hope on a daily basis.

Though I am Christian, this book is written as if I were speaking to a specific friend who is very angry with God. My friend hates God but she loves me. We are as different as two people could be, but we are bonded and united by our cancer. My writing is shaped by knowing her. I have leaned into the cancer community and positioned myself in the most hopeless situations. I have learned from each person I've encountered and have taken their struggles along with my own to create this book.

Many have traveled this cancering path, and some of us turned back to make your way a little smoother. We want you to know you are strong, capable, and full of purpose. You are not alone.

Introduction
I Am Lauren

INTRODUCTION
I Am Lauren

When I was thirty-five, I had been pregnant or nursing for six years. I had three beautiful, little, busy girls filling my life with laughter and chaos. Despite the lack of sleep and work of raising babies, when I finished nursing my third daughter, I began planning for a fourth child. This was when I found a lump in my breast. At the time, it didn't seem odd; my breasts hadn't been "normal" for years. Considering all the changes my body had been through with multiple pregnancies and years of nursing the girls, I didn't think anything of it.

Then, a few months later, the lump changed and started pushing up. At this point, I knew something wasn't right. When I think of the person I was then, there was no way I could have guessed how the decisions I made in these moments might change my life. I was young, healthy, and in the busiest season of my life. I was figuring out how to be responsible for children who required my attention every moment of the day. Caring for them was my most important job, yet I was also working full time. Concerns about my health were not my priority. I felt good. Life was moving forward just as it was supposed to, and cancer was the furthest thing from my mind.

When I noticed the change in the lump, I didn't know what to do. I spoke to my husband who asked me to get it checked out. Working full time and caring for three girls under five years old made this seem nearly impossible.

One day, I was picking my oldest daughter up from preschool, and there was a mammogram bus in the parking lot. I had my girls in car seats in the back of my car and pulled up to the bus. It was a pivotal moment that could have changed everything about our lives moving forward. I sat in that parking lot and wondered what I should do. I stared at the bus, and my mind filled with all the reasons why getting a mammogram that day wouldn't work. I was under forty, so I probably didn't qualify for a scan. I had three restless girls with me; someone on that bus would have to be exceptionally gracious and kind to go out of their way to entertain them while I walked through the process. Then my mind went to our nightly routine: dinner, bath time, homework, laundry. I don't remember the question ever emerging, "What if this is cancer?" I don't remember asking myself if it was best for my family to get that scan. I never considered what the outcome might be if this lump was dangerous. I was young, so the risks of this terminal disease never showed up in my decision-making. My motivation for getting a scan that day was strictly informational and a desire to honor my husband's wishes. At that moment, information could wait. As I sat there, I resolved my husband would understand if I waited and got it checked out later.

After weighing all the scenarios that I could imagine, I finally pulled out of the school's parking lot because the restlessness of the girls was becoming greater than the restlessness of my thoughts. I drove home and didn't think about the lump again for five months.

We moved from Tennessee to California at the end of that school year. It was an exciting and busy time. We took a cross-country trip, started new jobs, and bought a house. Then, five months after I sat in that parking lot staring at the mammogram bus, I started thinking about a fourth baby again. I decided to see a doctor since the lump had not gone away. I mentioned the lump, and my new primary care physician didn't say much. He didn't have any words of wisdom for me and wanted to send me to a specialist.

It was the nurse that day who stepped in. She told me of an excellent doctor, found me the information for that doctor, and sent me off with good wishes. I called that doctor, and she had one opening. I said, "That opening won't work for me, I have young children and—" She cut me off. She said if I was going to be her patient, I had to make a commitment. If I was not going to do the right thing for myself, she would not be my doctor. This statement is the moment my perspective changed. This gynecologist would not allow the needs of my family to keep me from understanding what was happening in my body.

A few weeks later, the specialist took one look at my breast and jumped into action. Within a few days, the doctor made appointments to ensure I had several scans done.

I had a feeling my life was about to change. So, on the morning of November 11, 2015, I put up Christmas decorations and made the girls wear Santa hats. We sat on the front porch of our new house and took Christmas pictures. In that picture, the girls are little and silly, my hair is long, and my husband, Clifton, looks solemn and steadfast. I wanted to capture the last moments of our innocence, the moments when joy came quickly. I didn't know what the scans would show, but I suspected the joy of our youth might fade that day.

Clifton and I drove an hour to the imaging center; he was with me every step of the way. When I was done with the tests, it was late in the evening, long after a doctor's office should be closed. I walked out of the imaging center, crossed the parking lot, and my phone rang just as my hand reached for the car's door handle. The doctor was on the line and asked me to come to her office.

The doctor had waited for me, suspecting the lump was cancer. She wanted to be there for me the moment my scans were complete. She didn't want to waste a day or even a moment.

Her office was quiet. Everyone had gone home for the night. She said the words, "You have cancer." She said that cancer would consume one year of my life. My kids were two, four, and six. I couldn't even imagine being bed-bound for one day, let alone one year. She said she was a cancer survivor, and she told me of her treatments. I walked out of her office, and when I got to the car, I began to cry. I couldn't get into the car because I was overwhelmed by my tears. I stood in the parking lot with my husband holding me. And my cancer journey began.

I went through every typical treatment for stage three estrogen-positive breast cancer for the next two years. I had chemo, the red devil kind. I had daily radiation that left me depressed and crying. I had a double mastectomy with the removal of lymph nodes that left me breastless and flat for six months. I honestly thought I did not want reconstruction. I didn't think of myself as self-conscious, but I couldn't look at myself in the mirror during those six months. Something in my subconscious set off alarms every time I saw myself. My emotions could not accept this flat-chested version of me as normal or acceptable, it felt wrong. I didn't want to see myself without my shirt on, and I didn't want my husband to see me unclothed. At the same time, my eyebrows and hair were still missing, leaving me bare in every possible way. To lose one's hair is an expected side effect, but once your eyebrows are missing along with your hairline, no resemblance of you seems to remain. There are no identifying marks. There is a reason they made Voldemort look the way he does; it is unnerving and scary. That is how I looked. My face and body left me unsettled and afraid. I was the physical manifestation of losing my identity, and every day I had to stand before myself, learning to let everything I knew disappear.

Because I never grew comfortable with my flat chest, and the radiation had damaged that skin so severely, I had a DIEP flap reconstruction. This type of reconstruction is one of the most extreme. When considering whether this surgery was right for me, I thought, "If I can have five good years with these good results, then it will all be worthwhile." The DIEP flap surgery took part of the healthy tissue from my stomach area and used that tissue to build new breasts. The old tissue on my chest was severely damaged from radiation, even limiting the mobility in my arms. This new skin allowed the doctor to remove the damaged skin and develop new breasts for me.

My plastic surgeon is a genius. I tell him this every time I see him, even years later. He took living flesh with living vessels and sculpted me so that I felt as if I had been restored. I am thankful for him. However, the surgery took a long time, and the stress of the surgery revealed that chemo had damaged my heart. As a result, the first night after surgery, I had cardiac complications. It was a terrifying situation with a room full of doctors and nurses, yet no one seemed sure about how to care for my heart. They were able to stop my heart and start it again without damaging my newly sculpted skin. That surgery proved to be too much for my heart, and now, without medication, my heart continues to flutter and race.

Like the choice to have a complicated surgery for the sake of long-term satisfaction, during my stage three treatments, I chose the most aggressive treatment plan. I told myself, "If cancer could emerge in my first twenty years after puberty, I would need to stop it from coming back in the next twenty years." I pushed my body in every possible way to ensure the cancer was in my past.

The final step in my stage three treatment schedule was the preventative removal of my ovaries. Less estrogen meant less food for cancer cells.

Before my surgery, I had a last-minute PET scan, a routine wrap-up procedure. It was December 2, 2017, the last day of school before Christmas break. I had my scan in the morning and then rushed home to prepare our house for fifteen second graders who had been invited over to watch a Christmas movie in their pajamas. My kitchen counters were covered in powdered sugar, the appetizers were on the table, and I had just pulled a batch of sugar cookies from the oven when my phone rang.

I answered it.

Christmas lights twinkled from every inch of my home, and my children danced to the music in the air. The house was filled with Christmas bliss, that peak of joy children experience when all responsibilities are gone, and nothing but the magic of the holiday is visible.

On the phone was my oncologist, but she was silent. Finally, she said, "I shouldn't be calling you, not now, not before the holidays, they teach us not to do this, but . . ." Then there was only silence until she could bring herself to say, "I'm sorry. I'm so sorry. You are so young."

She didn't say anything else, she didn't need to. I knew that my life would never be the same.

I set the pan of cookies on the counter and rushed to my room. The room was black as night. The darkness of the room hid me and enveloped me. I wept. I wailed. There was no reason to hold anything back. My life had just ended—it had been taken from me.

I don't know how long I wept in the darkness. I remember a neighbor opening my bedroom door and saying she was taking my children to her house. I remember my husband's presence, but mostly I remember the darkness. I had been diagnosed with stage four metastatic breast cancer, and only one thing filled my mind—I am going to die.

When I was diagnosed with stage three cancer, I was told that cancer would be a year of my life, then I would get back to doing all the things a young woman plans to do. Cancer was supposed to be a pause in life and nothing more. Those words are a carrot on a stick to get you through treatments, but they hold no truth. Cancer is never "one year of your life." No matter what stage of cancer impacts you, life is never the same.

Most women living with metastatic disease have a similar diagnosis story. It is not a story we like to tell. We don't write about it in our Christmas cards or discuss it on social media. To direct our thoughts to that moment is to relive its trauma. And to relive the breaking of our identity is too much to ask. The first moment of trauma is the moment that changes everything.

Fyodor Dostoevsky said, "There is only one thing that I dread: not to be worthy of my sufferings." The first three months after my diagnosis, I did not know if I could carry my suffering. The entire world was dark. Everywhere I looked, I saw a future lost. Around every corner was the next blow.

To receive a terminal diagnosis is to mourn for one's own life. I mourned through my uncertainty. I mourned for my children. I mourned for the experiences that would be lost, the life I would not live, the days unseen, and the burden of treatment with its finite list of options that might free me from this diagnosis.

My mourning began to be expressed through a desperate need to make the process easier for my children and husband. Every day, I went through a checklist in my mind of ways to establish their lives so that the loss of me would hurt them less. I began to write funeral instructions and letters. I became consumed by the process. I had already been through all standard-of-care treatments for stage three breast cancer, and they did not work. I was young, apparently treatment-resistant, and I felt hopeless. Hopelessness mixed with fear, and my thoughts grew increasingly narrow every day. After a week, my thoughts were consumed by one topic: my death.

Each day, I would take my girls to school and then come home to prepare the arrangements for my death. I cleaned out my closet so no one would need to decide what to do with my stuff. I made three piles, one for each girl, and began to sort my meaningful items. I took my jewelry to a local artist and asked him to take all my things and design three legacy rings for the girls. I sent my funeral instructions in an email to friends so my husband would have a plan in place when the time came.

I woke up every day, sat on the edge of my bed, and went down the list of what would need to be done for the day I would no longer be a part of my family.

I kept this routine for ten weeks.

One morning I woke up, and the burden of death was heavy on my mind. Everything felt veiled in darkness. As I sat on my bed, I felt stuck. I was not sure why I was getting out of bed anymore. I just sat in silence, not sure how to go on. Then, in my mind, I could see a child's sketch of a swirly tornado, lines going in continuous circles, larger at the top and small at the bottom.

As the tornado drawing went downward, the lines became more smudged until they were a blurred dark cloud. I could see myself being pulled downward. I could recognize that my thoughts grew darker and darker, and the further down I traveled, the less I could find a path of any kind. And the idea came to me that if I continued down this path, I would be pulled so deep into the depths of the tornado I would not be able to escape the darkness.

I paused to consider this reality and looked at my life over the past ten weeks. I considered my relationships and what I had accomplished. I reflected on my life. If I continued down this path, where would it take me, and what would my children learn from me?

Then, as if inspired, I looked upward toward the top of the swirly tornado in my mind. I could see the light, and everything felt less restricted. Moving upward in the tornado meant my life could get bigger and more significant rather than growing steadily smaller. I sat on the side of my bed and considered what I could accomplish if I moved upward.

At that moment, I had a revelation—a thought that still holds true today. If I live every day preparing to die, my life has already lost its impact. My story halts today because I will never move toward anything other than death itself. On the other hand, if I choose to focus on anything else, I could perpetually be moving upward, outward, away from darkness and the tunnel of fear.

That morning, I was paralyzed, sitting on the side of my bed, deciding who I would be—agree with fear and live within a statistic or be irrationally optimistic and embrace anything imaginable.

I could not find a reason to agree with fear and death. The fruit of a life of fear would never provide my family with anything except sadness, bitterness, and loss. So, I shifted my mind toward irrational hope. I had no reason to hope. My scans were not good, and my meds had not started impacting the tumors, but I could feel a potential found in hope that fear could not provide me. Perhaps hope could move me toward a brightness, a lighter burden, a purpose. With this in mind, I chose to embrace irrational hope. I had no reason or logic behind the decision, except hope made me feel like I could breathe. It made me closer to the person I wanted to be. Hope helped me shift my focus and pulled me out of the darkness.

Even as I began to rise from the bed, at that very moment, doubts about this new frame of mind set in. I shook my head and reassured myself that I wanted to focus on what was possible, no matter what the outcome might be.

I first chose to believe in a different set of possibilities, but I had to retrain my thought patterns. Initially, I had to check myself every few minutes to remain committed to the process. Over time, believing in the best-case scenario in every situation became my default mental response. I have so many amazing stories about how life super-exceeded my expectations because I took the risk of believing in a best-case scenario.

I am so thankful for that paralyzing moment at the side of my bed. In overcoming my fear of death, I found the tools to overcome my fear of just about anything. Instead of fear, irrational optimism has become my dominant mode of thought. Just as that swirly tornado sketch predicted, my thoughts continued to spread outward, and today I dwell on the possibility of what can be. Now I can see if I had chosen to remain in that dark tunnel, I would have wasted years. I would never have taken the risk of starting a nonprofit, a podcast, a book project, and so much more.

Over the next few years, my cancer felt like a roller coaster. One month my scans would show new growth, and the next, that new growth was gone. It took years before good scans happened, and then after three years of no evidence of disease, cancer began to grow again.

No matter what happens in my body, I have had years of life—years I could have wasted. If I had spent years betting on the worst-case scenario, I would have missed the opportunities unfolding around me daily.

Consider taking a risk today. Believe in irrational optimism. Irrational optimism is impactful because, despite the scans, you can genuinely believe something else is possible.

Believe in restoration. Believe you will leave the most significant legacy you can imagine. Believe in health and healing. Believe in relationships perpetually growing stronger, happier, and more fulfilled. Believe in what can be, then move toward an intentional, irrationally optimistic future daily.

The Dream of What Can Be

Antonio Machado said, "Traveler, there is no path. The path is made by walking." Irrational optimism permits me to create a path that takes me where I want to be tomorrow. I do not know the way, I do not know how to get there, and no explanation or certainty gives me direction. There is only hope, and the walking out of that hope.

I am a woman, mother, wife, sister, teacher, coach, researcher, advocate, leader, chef, and free Uber driver for my kids. I am this and so much more. Yet following my diagnosis, I set all of these other purposes aside for ten weeks, and I chose to live a life fully defined by a diagnosis. I sacrificed the joy found in the present because of the loss I would someday experience. Fear is like that; it smudges the lines between where you are and where you might be. When I rose from the bed that day, I chose to live in a way that was true to me. I now live with an intense purpose, demonstrating in every moment the legacy of life. My voice may begin frail, but stirring below the surface is the force of that tornado inside me.

I couldn't live boxed inside data-based boundaries. I had no choice but to embrace another perspective. Irrational optimism was required to balance the depth of my fears with lofty potential. I began to dream of change, strength, books I might write, and programs I might develop. I knew there was potential in me that had not been fully realized. I envisioned myself on a stage where I had a voice because of my weakness—my terminal diagnosis. I dreamt of helping others and of how I might shine a spotlight on the hope that could be found in the middle of despair. These visions moved me toward the person I wanted to be.

In 2018, I founded a nonprofit, Adventure Therapy Foundation, and I did so without any qualifications, except for a burning purpose in my heart. I designed an app that, once fully developed, will change the experience of cancer. I wrote a book, the one you are reading now. These things exist because of hope—hope that overcame fear.

Purpose

The purpose of this book is to acknowledge the typical emotional burdens that are found in the cancer experience. Here, I will provide a common language expressing the cancer experience. This is necessary because, at this time, we do not understand that there is a typical emotional response to cancer. We have never explored our experiences, so we don't fully understand the similarities we all share.

I am not a psychiatrist. I want that to be clear. I have no degree that positions me to speak on this topic. I write this book to begin a conversation that has previously been unspoken. How does cancer impact us? How do we emerge from it scarred but adventurous? Looking at this moment in history,

I recognize how I have been uniquely positioned. I may be among the first generation who will live with cancer. I am among the first of those who will live with metastatic disease with a high enough quality of life that I can wrestle with my questions and find some answers before cancer overcomes me. Because I will be among the first to find answers to these questions, I feel it is my duty to present you with what I know about the cancer experience.

When we begin cancer treatments, we are given a massive binder with the physical side effects of the medications we will take. Then, when we experience nausea or fatigue after chemo, we don't suddenly become concerned about a separate disease causing us to be tired all the time. The newness of the fatigue and nausea is understood to be the result of the treatment. We realize that others have experienced the symptoms mentioned in the treatment binder. Therefore, our experience is typical and even expected. The fear of these new symptoms is erased before it begins.

Unfortunately, there is no treatment binder for the typical emotional responses of cancer. There is no reference guide to what is typically experienced by millions of cancer survivors. Just because no manual has been provided, doesn't mean the emotional impact of cancer isn't experienced time and time again by survivors worldwide. Just as typical physical side effects are defined for treatment by common experiences, this book outlines the typical emotional side effects of cancer as defined by the stories of hundreds of survivors and co-survivors. These experiences demonstrate a "typical" emotional response to cancer.

This book is a first attempt to acknowledge and define the emotional side effects of cancer. I hope by describing these emotional experiences as typical, I will eliminate unnecessary fear, shame, and brokenness, and will expedite the emotional healing of cancer for all who will be diagnosed after me.

May this book be a swirly tornado that grips you until hope emerges.

Part 1
The Emotional Side Effects of Cancer

THE EMOTIONAL SIDE EFFECTS OF CANCER

Over the years, Adventure Therapy Foundation has served hundreds of people. The first thing we do when we meet these patients and survivors is ask to hear their story. Whether or not those impacted by cancer know it, their cancer story is usually on the tip of their tongue. When they call and meet someone who honestly wants to listen and help, a story is released in a flurry of emotion. A safe peer-to-peer space is invaluable. This safe space often allows those impacted by cancer to unexpectedly release much more than they knew they were carrying.

As we listened, it didn't take long for us to hear patterns in these stories. Each person who reached out to us assumed they were the only ones who had ever needed such answers. Yet the more we listened, the more apparent the connection was between the stories of these patients and survivors. It didn't seem to matter where a patient lived or what type of treatment they received; the correlations remained. So we began to take note of the connecting points—the difficult emotional burdens and the healing process. Once these connecting points were identified, we began to acknowledge and affirm how these experiences were a "typical response to cancer." Furthermore, we began to encourage their emotional journey through cancer and advise them on what they might expect in the next season of emotional healing. In this book, we want to do the same for you.

Three connecting points we have identified in the stories of those living with cancer are the presence of fear, isolation, and a broken identity. These three experiences are not unique to the cancer experience. They are universal to the human experience. In fact, they are present even in the earliest stories told of humanity.

In the book of Genesis, the story says:
Then the man and his wife heard the sound of the Lord God as he was walking in the garden in the cool of the day, and they hid from the Lord God among the trees of the garden. But the Lord God called to the man, "Where are you?"

He answered, "I heard you in the garden, and I was afraid because I was naked; so I hid."

. . .

So the Lord God banished him from the Garden of Eden to work the ground from which he had been taken. After he drove the man out, he placed on the east side of the Garden of Eden cherubim and a flaming sword flashing back and forth to guard the way to the tree of life. (Genesis 3:8–10, 23–24, NIV)

We see these three responses when Adam and Eve first eat the forbidden fruit. When God confronts them on their dinner choice, they:
- are afraid
- hide
- are exiled from the garden

Fast forward to 2019—fear, isolation, and a broken identity were also experienced globally during the COVID-19 pandemic. The world was filled with uncertainty, and there emerged a culture of fear. Even when no threat of COVID-19 was present, people remained afraid. During the pandemic, we were isolated. We quarantined and spent a significant amount of time staying home, away from others. The pandemic also changed our habits, our jobs, and our expectations. It changed how we ate and what we did for entertainment. All of these routines and expectations of life shifted our identity.

These three responses to life have been present throughout history, yet they continue to surprise us. When life shifts unexpectedly, fear, isolation, and a broken identity impact our mental health. Though we have countless opportunities to establish tools for these responses, they remain unfamiliar. Instead of learning to respond to uncertainty, we react by grasping desirable circumstances as quickly as possible. However, when life is disrupted by something as significant as cancer, rushing back into a life of certainty is not an option. Therefore, it is helpful to learn all we can about fear, isolation, and a broken identity. This book attempts to take a closer look at these three responses to uncertainty so that we may learn how to heal from trauma and become more resilient in the process. Let us take a closer look at each of them.

CHAPTER 1

Fear

Let's take a moment to look at the experience of fear. Do you remember, in great detail, your first date or the first day of school? Why do you remember it so well? Fear. In those moments, you feared rejection, making mistakes, or even that you might discover a new trajectory for your life. Fear makes you aware of every aspect of the situation, even the wrinkles on your pants or the smudges on the wall. The information you take in becomes locked into your memory with heightened accuracy. The emotion of fear lives in a moment, waking your mind and providing a state of alertness. Fear can be a friend. It increases your emotions, creating a greater capacity for your senses. In the right moment, fear can be a gift.

This same kind of good fear exists in adventures of every kind. We pay a lot of money to experience fear. We go to a scary movie, ride a roller coaster, climb up the side of a mountain, and paddle down a river because this good fear is exhilarating. The experience of fear on our own terms makes us feel alive. It drives out every other thought, focusing the mind and providing a sense of accomplishment. We enjoy this type of fear and want to experience it again and again! So we search for another ride, another river, another moment to hold onto.

Fear reflects the circumstance in which it is experienced. The first examples of fear are attached to uncertain but positive situations. The fear experienced in those settings feeds off the potentially positive outcomes. The experience of fear on an adventure or a first date is attached to a choice. We chose to go on the roller coaster, so even in our fear, we have a sense of choice and control.

There are other experiences of fear. Fear in times of pain or threat of pain is not a choice, and there are no potentially positive outcomes. The best outcome is the possibility of minimizing or escaping from future pain. Since the experience of fear mirrors our circumstances, it can be challenging to overcome when our circumstances are painful, unexpected, or inescapable.

Cancer and fear go hand in hand. Cancer is unexpected and inescapable. It causes uncertainty, trauma, risk, threat, sudden change, an unclear future, and present danger. Understandably, someone with a cancer diagnosis will experience fear. A fearful response to a cancer diagnosis is a natural and wise reaction. That's right, fear can be good for us because fear of cancer gets us to take action! Treatments are not easy, fun, pleasant, or desirable. Still, our fear of cancer is greater than our fear of cancer treatments. So fear becomes a motivation that helps us make difficult decisions and receive uncomfortable treatments. There is a time when we need fear to help us follow doctors' recommendations and show up to the infusion lab. Unfortunately, the fear of cancer does not stop there.

Life is made of layers of ever-changing circumstances, relationships, and decisions. Cancer is one circumstance. The fear of cancer can motivate us to act in the circumstances surrounding our cancer and its treatments. During treatment, fear can keep us safe. When we have a heart flutter or tingling in our fingertips, we take notice because fear has heightened our senses. With this heightened awareness, we can report potentially dangerous side effects to our doctors. However, fear likes to grow. The problematic thing with fear is that it doesn't like boundaries. When we allow fear to define more than our experience of difficult treatments, it will begin to encompass everything experienced in cancer. This fear stretches its arms and legs and starts running laps around all aspects of our lives. This empowered presence of fear begins to impact our relationships, and decisions. Fear is not a stagnant thing, nor is it an innocent bystander. As fear grows, it becomes a filter we see the world through. The longer we allow it to remain, the more control it has over our present and future lives.

We must take an honest look at the fear in our lives. Is the fear we experience based on a current threat or has fear become a part of our culture?

Perpetuated fear is a choice, even if it is a passive choice. Choosing to live in fear is a perspective that causes us to base our decisions on a potential worst-case scenario. This perspective causes us to consider a negative result that might occur in the future. Then we choose to align ourselves with that negative outcome before it has occurred. The choice to fear what has not occurred creates a mental culture of fear.

We must take an honest look at our thoughts, as fear is more detrimental to legacy than cancer. It will continue limiting, restricting, and debilitating life long after cancer treatments conclude.

Fear is also contagious. When we choose to live in fear after the threat has passed, we create a culture of fear in our households. By living in fear, we teach those we love to live in fear. Our own thought patterns, decisions, and willingness to embrace risk becomes a visible expression of fear that our children, loved ones, and friends respond to. We can teach others to limit their expectations in life by allowing fear to continue in ours. This is how fear can destroy our legacy.

Cancer is a disease of the body. Its greatest power is to limit the length of time we have on earth. Cancer's impact is limited to the body. A person can remain joyful, celebratory, loving, and kind while experiencing cancer. Cancer may limit our opportunities to express love but cannot impact our ability to embrace love, hope, or joy. On the other hand, fear will cause disease in the body, mind, and soul.

I talk with my girls about this often. The lesson is so important that I do not want it to go unnoticed. I ask them, "When I was in my early treatments for cancer, I lost my hair. Was I still your mom when that happened?"

They say, "Yes."

"During that same time, I had surgery and lost both of my breasts. Did I seem to become a different person because I had neither hair nor breasts?"

They say, "You were the same."

"Once, I had no eyebrows or hairline. I would look into the mirror and not recognize myself. Do you think I had become someone different because I couldn't recognize myself?"

They say, "You were still the same mom. You didn't change."

"Then I had so many surgeries and radiation. I lost some use of my arm from radiation, and some of my insides were removed. I had lots of scars and was very weak. Do you think these changes in my body also changed me?"

They say, "No matter what happened to your body, we still knew you loved us. To us, you were the same."

I tell them, "We are more than our bodies. My physical limitations do not limit my mind, heart, or spirit. Our appearance does not define who we truly are."

To have this conversation with my girls, I had to truly believe it about myself. If I had spoken this to them but lived in a completely different manner, they would not believe me, and my lesson would disappear.

Parenting through cancer is a difficult task. We are being watched all the time. Our emotions impact our children. The presence of our children through our cancer experience can provide a healthy level of accountability. What do we want them to believe about life? Whatever that may be, we must also believe it and live it. Where we waver, so will they. When we live by example, our children will learn how to face difficulties in their own lives.

Irrational Optimism

Fear creates tunnel vision. It limits what we can see, imagine, and do. When fear enters an uncertain situation, darkness settles in, eliminating our options. Tunnel vision forces us to look directly ahead toward the painful outcome designed by our fears. This one pain point is spotlighted while darkness blankets all other options. When fear is eliminated, blinders come off, and a horizon of interconnected opportunities can be found. This moment is often followed by the thought: How come I never thought of this before? Such a simple solution, and yet I couldn't see it.

Fear and cancer seem to go hand in hand. I don't remember when I was taught to fear cancer, yet my world shattered the moment I was told, "You have cancer." I didn't have to think about what it meant or sit and process how I felt. I knew I was terrified. I don't have any relatives impacted by cancer, and before my diagnosis, I never knew anyone in treatment. Without any personal experience, there I was with my fears defining every thought and every decision. It seems that by pursuing a greater awareness of cancer, we have also created a greater fear of it.

The fear of cancer is not rational. In the past ten years, the number of life-saving medical breakthroughs that have been discovered and released outnumber all research and treatment before now. So with these fantastic opportunities helping us live longer with cancer, shouldn't the fear of cancer be in decline? No! Fear does not adhere to logical boundaries. The fear of cancer continues to grow, and it will continue to do so, impacting generations despite the advancement of science. The only way for fear to be minimized is for us to intentionally choose a different approach in how we speak of and live with cancer.

A cancer diagnosis leaves a person with two choices: live in fear or choose joy. Joy does not seem like a natural alternative to fear. I had always considered courage to be the opposite of fear. But upon close inspection, I found that not to be the case. My definition of fear is: a constricting emotional response to an expected negative outcome in the future.

Instead of courage being the opposite of fear, courage is actually similar. My definition of courage is: an expansive emotion toward an expected negative outcome that may occur in the future.

Both emotional responses are based on an expectation of a negative outcome. Why do we look into the future and expect bad things to happen? How much of life has been stolen away because we chose to align ourselves with a worst-case scenario? Isn't it just as easy to use our imaginations to create something beautiful and good? These are the results we truly want. If we truly want these things, why don't they appear in our daily thought patterns?

After close consideration, I found that the opposite of fear is actually joy. My definition of joy is: an expansive emotional response to an expected overwhelmingly positive outcome in every future situation.

That sounds like something I can support. I want to look to the future and be free to expect the best results! Life is filled with possibility and wonder; shouldn't I use my imagination to consider the best possible results? When I align myself with a negative outcome that has not yet occurred, I am shaped by perpetuated fear. When I align myself with positive outcomes, I become irrationally optimistic and joyful.

My definition of irrational optimism is: a mindset based in joyful expectation that every situation will be resolved with better than expected success. This mindset is irrational because it does not need evidence or proof of pending success. It intends to point a person toward any potential opportunity that will allow the person to experience success to the greatest extent possible.

Learning to restore our imaginations will shift our mindsets to expect good things. Doing so activates a different part of our brains and releases healing hormones. Our thoughts are feeding our bodies, so what we imagine teaches our bodies what to expect.

Our mindsets directly impact our physical health. Whether we are living from a perspective of fear or joy, our mental perspective directly impacts our health outcomes. The choice is ours. Using our imaginations to consider the adverse outcomes is a habit with consequences. Negative thoughts release chemicals in our bodies that lead to negative health outcomes, and joyful thoughts lead to positive health outcomes.

Joy and Identity

When we choose a joyful mindset, we are free to become purpose-driven people. When living in a fear-based perspective, our goal is to experience minimal pain in life. Therefore, all of our emotional strength is required to maintain a defensive stance. From a joy-based perspective, our goal is to live well, to find our purpose, and pursue our goals. In this perspective, life is exciting! We can imagine a life well lived. We can take risks. We can live in the realm of possibility. We can do this because we are free of backup plans and what-ifs. When we stop living from a fear-based perspective we can step into a purposed identity.

We cannot make decisions every day based on fear and purpose. These are two opposing trajectories. We are either running from pain or toward purpose. When life is pulled by fear and by purpose, we come to a place of inaction. If we cannot resolve which of these paths to follow, we will become stagnant, unable to ever feel safe from the pain we fear, and unable to embrace our identity.

When we choose a joyful or irrationally optimistic perspective, our choices in life come into focus. Ninety-nine percent of the options available to us do not align with our unique purpose and, therefore, will become irrelevant. This makes life simpler (not the same as easier), less stressful, and more efficient.

But if we have yet to identify our most authentic identity or purpose, every available choice is an overwhelming distraction that diminishes our satisfaction. A lack of satisfaction due to the number of decisions available in a day causes us to return to a fearful posture.

Consider the number of decisions you make in an hour, day, or week. In those decisions, how many of them do you intentionally align with your identity? Visualize the version of yourself you dare to hope for, the person you believe you were designed to be. Now consider the decisions before you: What will I eat or wear? How should I use my time? Where should I spend my money? These three decisions really define most of life, yet how often do we look at these questions and align them with the person we want to become? How do my food or clothes impact my identity? How does my use of time impact my identity? How does where I spend my money impact my identity? These are significantly important questions, though because we make them repeatedly, they are often overlooked.

Creating opportunities for daily decisions to become the building blocks of your identity requires a quiet mind free from outside influences. Due to the constant input of media and marketing, a quiet mind is not easily achieved. If you have trouble quieting your mind, take time to listen to what is happening in the background noise of life. Are the stories you hear in your mind fear-driven? Are they stories of responsibility? Do you hear patterns of lacking? Not enough time, money, friends, or joy? Is there chatter in your mind that excites you? Are there visions of great and beautiful things? Taking note of these internal conversations informs us of our subconscious motivators.

Fear and Uncertainty

Fear and uncertainty are not the same. Uncertainty is a result of our lives bumping up against circumstances outside of our control. Fear, on the other hand, is an emotional response. It happens inside us, for a moment, as we process something unexpected or unknown.

After a cancer diagnosis, we must increase our capacity to live with uncertainty. We are living in an age of information where it is easy to get the answer to many of our questions. Yet some questions are too complicated to ever be answered. To increase our capacity for uncertainty, we must recognize some questions will go unanswered for a season. Though there is no immediate answer, we must still ask them. Asking questions acknowledges our hearts. It brings clarity to our experience. Asking a question helps us process what our hearts truly want.

By writing down our questions, we can observe patterns of uncertainty. These patterns will show us a more profound concern.

exploring the seasons of emotional healing

Those deeper places tend to send out many questions because they hold our values. Our hearts often want to know less about what tomorrow will bring and more about whether we can continue to live in a way that reflects our true selves. When we write down our questions, the questions themselves bring us clarity. The patterns in our questions reveal the longing of our hearts.

A five-year-old child is curious about everything. This is exhibited through a million questions a day. Our brain feels like a five-year-old's when it comes across a new situation—like a cancer diagnosis—it is curious about everything. Our brain tries to make sense of the situation because it recognizes a threat and is trying to protect us through knowledge. Unfortunately, few definitive answers are available to ease the mind's hunger for certainty. Therefore, the best thing we can do is listen to the questions. Like a five-year-old child, if we don't listen to those questions, they will get asked repeatedly. Trust what your kindergarten teacher said, and remind yourself, "There are no dumb questions." Our questions and curiosities are meaningful even if an answer cannot be readily found. Unasked questions take root and trigger fear.

FEAR ≠ UNCERTAINTY

Uncertainty is just what the word says, not being certain, not knowing what to expect, not knowing the best answer.

Fear is how your heart responds to the lack of information.

Remember, fear and uncertainty are not the same. Fear is an emotional response, while uncertainty is tied to the search for a predictable outcome. Uncertainty resides in our heads, fear lives in our hearts.

Take Action

Let's engage in practicing a shift in perspective. To transition from a fearful or tunnel perspective to a hopeful or horizon perspective, you must know which perspective you are currently in. Self-reflection and honesty help us know where we are and where we want to be. A tunnel of fear means I cannot see any options other than what I am fearing. When looking into the future I see darkness and that which I fear, and nothing more. As long as I remain in this perspective the reality of this mindset feels real and unavoidable. The fearful tunnel perspective makes me feel trapped and even doomed to remain stuck inside one experience.

No take a deep breath. Do it again and again. Rest your mind.

Sit in a mentally resting position until your mind is at peace. Give yourself time to let go of your questions and fears.

Move your mind away from any urgency you feel. Notice if there is any tightness in your body or mind.

exploring the seasons of emotional healing

Take a deep breath and wait until you relax.

Imagine a new perspective, a hopeful, beautiful scene. Allow that scene to represent your life. Your life is a horizon. Allow this horizon to spread out before you. Follow the view as it expands.

Think of what it means for your life to exist on this horizon. Your life does not exist in a tunnel but is a vast, expansive horizon filled with interlinking parts. Consider the mundane tasks and the people who pass through your day. In your mind, take these simple daily occurrences and picture them as the wind and birds that fly across the horizon. They are present but almost unnoticed in their common nature. Look at the way the wind impacts the birds. Consider how the birds bring change in their environment. Each bird is creating a uniquely beautiful possibility found in seeds and pollen. Consider the birds and the winds of your life; these small, fleeting moments bring change. Consider how each breeze can bring new possibilities and how each gust of wind that passes through your life is doing important work for connecting you to those around you. Small shifts in your life can open an entirely new set of opportunities. Imagine what those opportunities look like.

Consider all the good that has occurred to create this horizon. Ponder the impact of your constantly expanding life.

Take a deep breath and continue your day with this new mindset.

REFLECTIONS

First Steps Toward a New Direction

When I experience fear, it feels like a squeezing pressure in my breath that moves to my shoulders and eventually my mind. When it reaches my mind, it feels like I am wearing blinders. I can only see the one scenario that scares me the most. I feel like I am moving through a tunnel and have no escape because I must move in one direction only. There are no choices, only forced outcomes. I can't find a way out of my situation. I become dogmatically convinced that the negative outcome is the only possible outcome. My eyes are captured by an opening at the end of the tunnel. Except, in the case of fear, it isn't a welcoming light; it is what I fear the most in a particular situation. My body tenses and my heart begins to race. My relationships also become tense, and I run about my day trying to escape the one scenario I can't seem to get around.

It was challenging when I decided to live with a different perspective on cancer. I had so much practice being afraid of cancer that it was hard to see any other way. I had to unlearn what had been so easy to accept and teach myself an entirely new perspective. At first, I could barely grasp the concept. All I knew was I wanted to live differently. I remained focused on the outcome. I thought about the outcome or path I would walk if I stayed in fear, and then I thought of what would happen if I found a different perspective. I began with only moments, glimpses of another emotional state. I had to stop every negative thought and replace it with something hopeful.

At first, I could only stand in joy or gratitude for a moment before slipping back into fear. However, I remained vigilant. I wanted to walk a different path, so I found tools to redirect my mind. I used songs, scriptures, and quotes to help me focus.

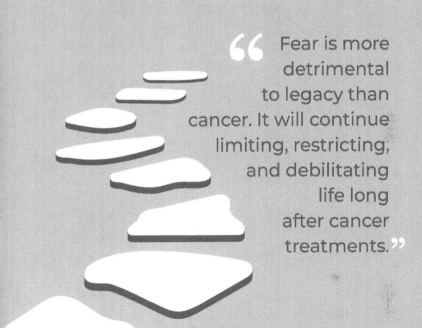

" Fear is more detrimental to legacy than cancer. It will continue limiting, restricting, and debilitating life long after cancer treatments. "

I cut out all triggers that would reestablish a fear-based mentality. Sometimes, those triggers were people. I was required to fight for my peace of mind.

Over time I could remain free of fear for days and weeks. There were some triggers I could not escape. I still had to go to the cancer center for treatment and scans. I had to take my daily medications and have regular lab work.

The most challenging trigger to overcome was that of a scan. "Scanxiety" ripped at my mind. Scans did not simply trigger future-based negative expectations, they returned me to where my trauma began. The color of the walls, the face of the receptionist, the smell of the building, and the taste of the water fountain all reminded me of how this cancer experience began. That cancer center held a whole bag of triggers while also making me question if this experience was about to start again.

In the days leading up to a scan, I might regress to taking my fearful thoughts captive every hour. On the drive to a scan, it was a moment-by-moment decision. I often had encouraging music playing louder than my thoughts (sometimes very loud). I often cried on the way to the scan, not out of fear but because of the struggle. I would weep because I wanted to believe what was so difficult to believe.

Perspective is a choice. I found the power to control what I believed. Cancer is a disease our culture fears. It seems automated for us to respond and remain in fear once we have been diagnosed with cancer. In fact, those around us expect us to live in fear! They might even embrace fear on our behalf. Letting go of fear is not a simple shrug-of-the-shoulders decision. The longer you make fear-based decisions, the more difficult this shift becomes. The longer our society fears cancer, the harder it will be for us to believe in a positive outcome.

Cancer requires that I endure hardships and face my mortality. I must acknowledge and embrace this experience as something that makes me stronger. I am resilient, tested by life's greatest test, yet I continue to live, and live well. The fear of cancer has pressed me in such a way that I am left with two choices: to be overcome by fear or to completely let go of fear. As I practice shifting my own perspective, I have found a gift. This choice grants me the power to overcome not just the fear of cancer, but all fear.

> **PERSPECTIVE *is a* CHOICE.**

CHAPTER 2

Isolation

COVID-19 gave each of us an intense dose of isolation. In 2020, the world shut down, and humanity was cut off from one another. In March of 2020, I picked my kids up from school, and we planned to head out the next morning for a road trip up the Pacific Coast. We went to bed with this plan in our minds and woke up the next day to learn of a lockdown order—no one should leave their home. It was a completely new idea. What happens if we do leave our home? Where is the threat? How can we keep our family truly safe? Everyone had different answers to these questions. I remember having friends over for dinner during this time. We sat outside, and everyone brought their own dishes to minimize contamination. There was a curfew in place, so even before we had finished eating, our friends felt the need to rush home to ensure they were not caught out after the curfew.

Since we were staying home, we began hanging out with our neighbors in the yard. We sat with chairs ten feet apart, attempting to remain in our own yards to ensure we did not break any state restrictions. We drew circles on the sidewalks and told the kids to stay inside of their circles to ensure they remained at a "safe" distance. We separated ourselves physically from everyone outside of our home. We took extreme action to protect ourselves from the unknown threat that could seemingly be found anywhere.

The world stopped, but we had comfort in knowing our lives had stopped together. The media showed clips of people worldwide finding new ways to connect during the pandemic. We knew that no matter how difficult this moment felt, others understood. No matter where we were located, the isolation was the same for us all.

This global pandemic educated the world about the emotional impact of disease. The emotional impact of isolation became evident, and we will continue to see the ripples of this impact for many years.

Isolation in cancer is a similar experience, but it is different. It is harder than what we faced during COVID-19. In cancer, the beginning is the same. One day you have plans, and the next day those plans are erased. But they are only erased for you. Everyone else can move ahead with their lives, but you must suddenly stop. You begin to ask questions: How did this happen? How will I work? How will treatment change me? When will I get my life back? You ask these questions, just like you did during COVID-19, but no one else is asking these questions with you. In your physical isolation, you find yourself emotionally isolated as well. Those who love you don't understand. So you long for someone who can understand. A cancer survivor cannot be identified in a crowd, so those who might understand are hard to find.

The situation becomes more complicated as you find yourself in need of constant support. Your loved ones take on your responsibilities. They run errands, deliver meals, and help around the house. After doing all of your chores and their own, it doesn't seem appropriate to unload your emotional burdens on them as well. Plus, they have questions and concerns of their own, and your questions will only increase their burdens.

The circle of isolation increases. It turns acquaintances into strangers, frail relationships into acquaintances, and friendships into awkward silence. Very few people know how to lean into a crisis.

Isolation is an emotional side effect of cancer. Only you can walk through a treatment plan. Only you are facing your mortality. Only you are wrestling with your body, looking for signs of reoccurrence. Only you truly understand how cancer is changing you.

Isolation and Identity

It is strange to say that I have felt isolated even when friends and family were surrounding me. I have felt isolated even when my children were around me twenty-four hours a day, seven days a week. I have felt isolated at holiday gatherings and dinner parties. This type of isolation is tied to the shift in identity that occurs during the cancer experience. There is an unknowing of self that occurs. As we wrestle with the changes happening in ourselves, it is extremely difficult to feel known, acknowledged, or accepted.

I was diagnosed with cancer two times during the holiday season. My stage three diagnosis happened two weeks before Thanksgiving. We decided not to cause alarm among our family until we knew exactly what was happening with treatments. I remember being among forty or fifty family members and feeling all alone. They didn't know my life was changing. They

exploring the seasons of emotional healing

didn't understand the questions racing through my head. In some moments, I felt like I should make an announcement, and in other moments, I just wanted to hide. Even in the first weeks of my diagnosis, I felt cut off and isolated. I was experiencing something that no one in the room had experienced and no one in the room could fix for me.

My second diagnosis of stage four cancer was a week before Christmas. That Christmas was one of the worst moments of my life. I had to go through the holiday season of hope and joy when I felt hopeless and fearful. My family gathered, and my mom suddenly flew in. I felt broken off from everything. I sat in one area of the house, knowing that everyone else was sitting in another room getting their game plan together on my behalf. I didn't want to be with anyone, I didn't even want to be with myself. My life as I knew it was gone, and I didn't know where I fit into this space anymore. I was in a house filled with twenty-five of the people who loved me most, and I was so alone. No one knew what to say, so not once over our three-day Christmas gathering did anyone say the word cancer to me. They have told me now that cancer is all they spoke of throughout the whole of our holiday, just not to me. I left that weekend defeated. I spent three days with my family, yet isolation was all I experienced.

Isolation is a painful experience because we are designed to be connected and unified. Our physical bodies, emotional well-being, and spiritual health are dependent on belonging. In my experience, I had a supportive family during both of my diagnoses. However, cancer made me an outsider even in my own family. The isolation I felt left a wound that took time to overcome.

For many years after my diagnosis, I had a traumatic response whenever I was left behind. Once, a group was heading off to Walmart (not the most exciting of outings!), and I wanted to go but was not invited, and the emotion of these previous deeply isolating moments crept up. I felt the deep rejection all over again. My isolation wounds had not healed, and so every time I was left out, that wound throbbed, releasing old pain.

Isolation may not have anything to do with being surrounded by people. In the cancer experience, or any trauma, isolation can be a sign of our own shifting identity. We ask ourselves the question, "Where do I belong now that I am different?" Until we find an answer to this question, the experience of isolation remains.

In my situation, I had people who loved me, whom I belonged to just as I had belonged before my diagnosis. The change that occurred started inside of me, not in the number of people in my life. I needed something different, something more, but I did not know what I needed. My emotional and relational needs had changed because of cancer, but they changed only in me. My family went on being family, but at this moment, I felt rejected. Their laughter was painful, their distracted conversation made me angry. Every word felt purposeless because I was out of strength, and I needed someone to help take away my pain. I didn't know how they could do it, nor did they. So my isolation grew inside the crowd.

I felt this same isolation as a child when my parents divorced. It felt like such a scandal, and when I looked out at the world, I could see them looking back at me a little differently. My identity shifted as a child, just as it did in my cancer experience. This isolation is tied to a need to belong, to be known and acknowledged for who I truly am. This traumatic experience caused me to lose my understanding of who I was. Until my basic understanding of my own identity could be restored, no one at my side could diminish my feeling of isolation. Isolation must be healed from within before it can be resolved with others.

Isolation and Belonging

My cancer experience places me on a different path than most in my pre-cancer community. When I am at the school pick-up line and talking among the moms who gather there, I don't connect with their concerns or worries. When I listen to the conversations around me at my daughter's softball practice, I cannot relate to the emotions or priorities I see there. Of course, I have always been on my own path. However, before my cancer diagnosis, I felt that what made me the same as others was greater than what made me different. There was a possibility of being known, of fitting in easily, of feeling normal. Cancer makes that feeling of normalcy much more difficult to achieve. From the day I was diagnosed with stage four cancer, I never quite felt comfortable again. I have felt out of place in my body, my friends' groups, and my identity.

The cancer experience exaggerates an unmet need to belong. As we grow accustomed to isolation, we can begin to choose to isolate ourselves as a means of controlling this painful experience. This can be seen even within a community of people impacted by cancer, often there can be an unnecessary rift. Those impacted by stage one or whose treatments led to a timely resolution of cancer can feel they don't have the right to be embraced by the rest of those impacted by cancer. Those impacted by a terminal diagnosis often feel that only those with a similar taste of mortality can truly understand. While we constantly seek others who can acknowledge us at our deepest level, we put up barriers between ourselves and others as a means of controlling our disappointments. However, when we find others who can mirror our experience, a sense of normalcy returns. The cancer community should be a place of refuge. There should be no division among those with a cancer diagnosis.

When I speak with someone impacted by stage one cancer, I remind them that we don't say a woman is "a little pregnant" when she is in her first trimester. Just as a pregnant woman is truly pregnant from the moment of conception until birth, those of us living out a cancer experience are all fully impacted by cancer. The emotional side effects of cancer are the same for each of us. We experience different lines of treatment, but the emotional side effects of cancer remain the same for everyone who receives a cancer diagnosis, whether they are diagnosed with stage one or stage four. Our emotional side effects are the same because uncertainty around our future is a burden in our minds.

Education about the disease has taught us to associate cancer with death. This, of course, is not everyone's story, but we have been shown statistics and seen pictures of those sick from cancer to the extent that the association is unshakable. This association between cancer and death is present in the mind of anyone with a diagnosis. Similarly, this association is alive and well in the minds of those around us. While we wrestle with our own mortality, we find no refuge or hope from others in our lives. They, too, are often wrestling with the same information. Because we have been so well-educated, for better or worse, about the potential impact of cancer, it does not require an advanced cancer for us to experience uncertainty and fear for our future. For this reason, the emotional side effects of cancer are shared by all of those impacted by the disease.

Isolation is experienced for many reasons. We might choose isolation as a means of protection from disappointment. Sometimes isolation is even confused as a strength. When a proud statement like "I made it through without anyone's help" is declared, my heart sinks. I am confident a person or organization is present who wants to walk through this experience with you. I also know a gift can be received or rejected. Sometimes we are hurting too much to receive the gift of someone's presence.

Sometimes we choose isolation because we don't feel worthy. For whatever reason, isolation can, at times, be a choice.

Isolation as a Season

It is often through our tears that we discover hope. In our most profound hurts, we experience our soul's purpose. In isolation, we can discover a deep desire to belong. A desire that has always been present but is more profound. It requires too much energy to deny our deepest needs during our cancer experience. Therefore, this season of life is an opportunity for honesty with ourselves. When it comes to minimizing isolation, there is only one way forward. To satisfy this need, we must open ourselves to the world around us.

In each of the emotional side effects of cancer, there is a calling to a better way of being. Cancer brings us face to face with the emotions and wounds that we repressed before our diagnosis. While it is not pleasant to see fear, isolation, and a broken identity present in our lives, it is healthy. It is an opportunity to do the work of bringing healing into these areas.

Consider isolation a season of life that reveals who you are and what you want to be. Listen to your heart and take note of the people you long for. Pay attention to whom you are most disappointed with and who shows up the best for you. These insights provide you with a key to unlock your sense of belonging. Once you find this key, allow it to be a source of encouragement to you for the rest of your life.

Strength and Weakness

If we search for quotes about strength, we will find ancient wisdom passed down from every religion and region. The quotes do not talk about financial success or physical stature. Instead, they speak of how one only finds strength when living in a community alongside others, bonded in common dependency. Life is much more about our weaknesses than our strengths, yet we live as if the opposite were true. In weakness, we discover who we are. We are able to share the true essence of ourselves. In weakness, we can genuinely experience and receive kindness and love. On the other hand, strength creates a sense of independence or stature. Independent strength creates walls between us and everyone else, resulting in isolation.

We have a myth that strength is valuable above all else. This idea is so present in our society that even children will respond that they are "ok" when asked, no matter what is happening in their lives or minds. Why do we live in isolation, yearning for the closeness of a friend? Why is it nearly impossible to ask for help? Why do we allow stress to build up until we live with anxiety and heart attacks? Even when our bodies are demanding rest and assistance, our mouths will never admit a lack of strength.

Independent strength is a lie we have bought, taught, and sought even though the most significant product of strength is isolation.

Because of this type of strength, each of us sits on an island of isolation wishing for close friends, longing for someone to help carry the load. The truth is, there are plenty of someones sitting next door to you, hoping for the same thing. The person in front of you in line, in the cubicle across from yours, and in the park walking their dog are all choosing an island of strength, looking out at a world from which they are cut off—our facade of strength keeps us apart.

I would like to propose a change of perspective. Let's make weak the new strong. Weakness looks like a cancer survivor who cannot have children embracing a child who lost a parent, allowing love to flow forth from her wounds. Weakness looks

exploring the seasons of emotional healing

like a mother with stage four cancer welcoming others into her children's lives so the children may experience love and acceptance from a new source. Weakness looks like all of us examining our hearts, then allowing our brokenness to heal the brokenness in others. By using this type of strength, perhaps we can all find ourselves healed along the way.

An act of kindness can look like weakness. Kindness is an intentional investment in others. It builds the type of connection that every person craves. It is a cure for isolation and a bridge that eliminates individual strength. Kindness is a path toward resilience, not personal power, but a strength of purpose, a strength found in community, a strength with no thought of self. It requires time, money, or emotion, without guaranteeing personal gain. Therefore, kindness weakens the individual, but this individual sacrifice creates a strong sense of belonging.

The relationship between strength and weakness is a paradox. Our constant pursuit of individual strength has left us weak as individuals and as communities. Yet a willingness to embrace our weaknesses enables us to be fortified by the kindness of others and helps us build strong communities. It is in weakness that we can begin understanding the power kindness possesses.

I urge us all to investigate our own lives and ask ourselves these questions: Is the pursuit of individual strength best for me? What would I experience if I chose instead to pursue kindness and express my weakness authentically?

I walked the Camino de Santiago in 2022. This truth of needing others was never more evident than on this walk. After a week of strenuous walking, your brain is tired, senses are dulled, and sometimes you are on autopilot. One day I was walking in the rain, it had rained all day, and we were still hiking up mountains. Seeing the signs that gave us direction in the rain was difficult. There was a woman I had met on the trail who was walking alone. I saw the arrow, turned off the main road, and decided to wait for my fellow traveler. I stood there in the pouring rain and thought about how we need friends more than ever in the most challenging times to help us move forward in the right direction. All of us are doing our best. We are journeying through life, giving each day all that we have, but without friends in front of us or at our side, we could easily journey with all our might in the entirely wrong direction. I waited at that turning point and waved her onto the right path. She was in pain, her knees were tired, so I walked slowly, staying with her the rest of the day. We had great conversations and created new rhythms of walking that minimized her pain. She began the day with two travel companions. She had told those two companions to go on without her. In her weakness, she wanted to be strong, but that independence left her alone throughout a very difficult day. I am confident her friends would have stayed at her side if she had not chosen to be "strong" and send them on at their much quicker pace. Independent strength often leaves us alone, in pain, during our most difficult days.

Take Action

When cancer treatments end, your mind is exhausted. You have been making decisions you were not qualified to make for a long time. You are physically tired, relationally stretched thin, and might feel completely helpless to make meaningful decisions about who you want to be.

At this season, invite your family and friends to circle you. They have witnessed all you have endured. They were unable to carry your burden. They were unable to fix your problem of cancer. But they know and love you and can help you as you move forward. You may not choose to walk the same path you were on before cancer, but you will want to walk in a way that is true to who you are. Allow these people to guide you. Let them remind you of who you are, not who you were or what you do, but who you are. Let them speak of your strength (even if you don't feel strong) and your beauty (even if you don't feel beautiful). Let them restore you, and then invite them to help you find the way forward. Let them become markers on your path as you begin a new journey in life. The path back to who you were is broken and marred by the fires of life. The only way to start journeying is to move forward, stepping into the bright green emergent growth available in this new season of life.

REFLECTIONS
Redefining Who I Am

I have a huge family, so there is very little reason for me to ever feel alone. However, being alone and feeling isolated stems from different needs. Isolation comes from not feeling known, seen, or heard. Despite rarely being alone, I have struggled for many years with isolation. My cancer diagnosis was a catalyst for change in me. I suddenly had a deep urgency to live out what was most important. I could not chit-chat at a party about the weather or sports. I could not pretend to be interested in conversations about traffic or politics. Life felt so essential and so undervalued. The more I embraced the change in me, the more isolated I felt. It took four years for those surrounding me to begin to see who I was becoming. It was not their fault. First, I had to go through a season of learning for myself who I wanted to become. Then I had to put that vision of myself into words, again only for my understanding. Finally, I had to begin living my new identity. It was only when my actions changed that others had their first opportunity to notice the person I was becoming.

While wrestling with myself, my values, and my vision for the future, I was isolated. I wanted to be seen more than ever because I could barely see myself. I wanted to be heard more than ever because I needed a sounding board to help me clarify my thoughts. I needed to be known and encouraged in whatever risk I was about to take as I risked stepping into the identity I wanted to become. However, when wrestling with myself, I could not communicate any of this to the people around me. I could not ask for what I could not fully understand. All that shifting and redefining took time, and while I wrestled with myself and my identity, I felt incredibly isolated. No one else could see, hear, or know me while I was learning to see, hear, and know myself.

> Until my basic understanding of my own identity could be restored, no one at my side could diminish my feeling of isolation. Isolation must be healed from within before it can be resolved with others.

CHAPTER 3

Identity

Identity tells us who we are. Our image, what we do, and whom we belong to becomes an equation predicting life's trajectory. This equation gives us direction and certainty. We predict that if we adjust our input, the plot points of life will adjust in proportion to our life's equation, and our trajectory will make shifts in a desirable direction. We learn to rely on this equation and build our values, purpose, and worth around our identity equation and its trajectory.

Identity is so deeply established in our subconscious that it goes unnoticed. We do not know the extent we rely on it until it is shaken, deconstructed, or broken. Unfortunately, much of our identity is dependent upon our circumstances. The identity equation that predicts our expectations for life exists inside a chaotic, unpredictable world. The factors outside our control are greater in number and impact than anything we have inside our control. Despite our awareness of circumstantial chaos, this impact on our identity equation cannot be predicted. When the circumstances of life break our identity, we become aware of how we allow our identity equation to provide us with a false sense of security.

Cancer is one of those chaotic, unpredictable circumstances that forever alters a person's identity. It takes our expected trajectory and erases all known outcomes. Our identity is broken. The security of life is shaken. Our value and purpose come into question.

A broken identity is a typical emotional side effect of cancer. It is typical, meaning it is experienced by most people impacted by cancer and should be expected. Since cancer will impact identity, we need to understand it better.

Protecting Yourself from Identity Theft

In our digital age, we are provided with more entertainment input than we could ever exhaust: from social media to the hottest new streaming series, from following our favorite teams to shopping online, the opportunities to learn, connect, and be entertained are rushing toward us through alerts on our phones and banners across our televisions. And these opportunities never slow down. On top of this, opportunities to engage in new responsibilities fill our days. From social change to environmental change, and from responsibilities of the family to our careers, the pressure to respond to our world's needs fills our minds. Then, swirling among all of this is the fear that we should do more. Fear of change is perpetual, filling our minds and, in time, leading to mental and emotional paralysis. Fear keeps us from engaging and minimizes our impact. In a world filled with abundant opportunity, it is difficult to stop and look at who we are becoming. In the midst of all this, how is our use of life's limited resources and time shaping who we will become?

In the digital world, we take many precautions to protect our virtual identity from being stolen by criminals, but how much thought do we give to protecting our true identity? Just as we would take time to purchase identity theft insurance, shred all personal documents, or create unique and elaborate passwords for virtual interactions, we must develop rituals in life that preserve and protect our most authentic identity.

We are a society of Band-Aid solutions. We often fix how something looks because it feels uncomfortable, while forgetting to find the source of the pain. This is true about identity theft. When I drive on the freeway, dozens of billboards promise to protect my identity, while all of the other billboards are trying to sell me an identity shaped by what I purchase.

True identity theft is happening all the time. When we make a decision based on marketing or spend days "vegging out," our true identity is stolen. Passively allowing ourselves to become washed away by streaming abundance allows someone else's fictional life to replace our own. Protecting our identity increases our quality of life. It is knowing ourselves and experiencing confidence in every purposeful decision.

How would you define your identity? What steps do you take to protect it?

Protecting your true identity requires a system for capturing your deepest thoughts, feelings, dreams, and purposes. These hold your true identity. These quiet whisperings should frame every decision and perspective of life, but how often do you acknowledge them?

I have spent my lifetime journaling. I began journaling at a young age simply because I needed someone to talk to. This remained a common experience throughout my life. I typically have more thoughts than people listening to them. So in my journals, I write down everything. Even when I am out of the habit of writing, I always return to journaling when I find my mind cluttered with questions and fears. Living through the chaos of life makes it easy to be filled with questions. Questions left unprocessed can turn to fear. Whenever I feel fear emerging or sense my frustration is on a loop, I know I have some deeper thoughts below those emotions that need to be processed. Journaling allows me to uncover my deepest thoughts. It often takes time. I have to fully acknowledge my fears before I can look deeper into what might be stirring inside my cluttered mind.

Often, by journaling, hope is revealed. Hope that is unspoken or unrealized can lead me to disappointment, fear, and frustration. By journaling, I am reminded of what is at the core of my identity. I am reminded that I am not a person of fear or frustration, but instead, a person of hope.

While journaling works for me, there are many tools for protecting your true identity. Leaving yourself audio notes or sending yourself emails can be easy options that require nothing more than the phone in your hand.

The better we understand true identity, the more resilient we become. While at first glance, most of the factors in our identity equation are action based or external, the foundation of those decisions is much deeper. When we take the time to acknowledge and protect the deepest levels of our identity, we increase our resiliency. The chaos of life will break the outer layers of our identity, but if we have done the work to protect our identity at the deepest levels, we will remain confident in our innate value. This confidence allows us to become resilient.

I am reminded of a quote from the movie *Shrek*. When describing himself, Shrek says, "Ogres are like onions . . . Onions have layers." Our identity has many layers. When the outer layers of my identity become stressful or overwhelming, I use journaling as a tool to help me rediscover the deeper layers. The deeper I can see inside my own motivations, the less those motivations will be shaken by the chaos of life.

Journaling also brings me back to my heart's desires. Where do I feel my purpose? What part of my life has unshakable meaning? Understanding my personal purpose gives me strength that rises above every circumstance. This part of my identity might be the quickest piece of myself to be lost. My personal purpose is not lost or forgotten because of a lack of effort. In fact, nothing could be further from the truth.

From a very young age, I have had a strong sense of purpose. I want to change the world. I want to lead a nonprofit that speaks boldly. I have wanted this since high school. I remember listening to a panel discussion in college, it was a huge seminar room, and a panelist gave a call to action—leaders were needed. I sat in the crowd with tears running down my face. I would stand, leave family and friends, and do whatever it took to be that leader, to bring that change. That fire inside of me never faded. In every season of life, I felt as though I was sitting in that crowd with tears on my face because my heart was telling me to sacrifice comfort and certainty to make this world a little less broken.

Then when I was twenty-five, I met Clifton, and a few years later, I had my first daughter. The fire to change the world did not go out but was no longer my heart's only motivation. I could see a vision of creating a family and raising happy children. I underestimated the work required to fulfill this new vision! I soon began making decisions that were best for the family. I became a teacher and spent every waking moment working or caring for the girls.

Though I was not trying to lose my life's purpose by raising a family, I did find carrying two purposes was nearly impossible. Before long, I had a career that supported my family's schedule and financial needs. I could have locked that trajectory in and walked it out for the next twenty-five years. The problem was, I never felt fulfilled. I was good at my job but felt out of place. My life's purpose would not relinquish control of my heart despite this new career that made sense in every other way. Once I even quit my teaching job to make space for something new, but teaching opportunities tracked me down, making it difficult to pursue a new trajectory.

When I made trajectory-shifting decisions in the first thirty-five years of my life, I always thought it was best for myself and my family. I was not trying to deny my life's purpose. Despite those "best decisions," I continued to feel the call of something else. Something had a pull on my life even though I couldn't define it.

All through these years, I kept journaling. I asked my questions and dug deeper into my heart. When I did not feel fulfilled in my work, I would look deeper into my identity and ask why. I left multiple career paths, and each time I left, I was offered a raise or a better position as an incentive to stay. I knew what I did and how much money I made was not my true identity. I knew my true identity was not aligning with these career paths. I knew that to live a life without regret, I had to take the risk of following that calling until I found myself feeling the passion of that college student sitting in the seminar with tears rolling down her face.

Throughout this ten-year-long process, no one could answer these questions for me. No one could look deeper into my identity and find answers—no one except me. I needed to do a lot of journaling to find my direction. I had to repeatedly remind myself of who I was and what I wanted to become.

When I was diagnosed with cancer, it was the worst and best moment of my life. I knew I would live without certainty, and my health, and perhaps my life, would be compromised. At the same time, I knew I had found my voice. I found a space where I could bring change to a broken world.

My sense of purpose gave me strength in and through every circumstance. I spent my life pursuing a purpose-filled life. Through journaling, I had continued to peel back the layers of my identity. My identity was not in my motherhood or job. It was not about what I could do or how I looked. I had protected my identity, and when the chaos of a cancer diagnosis entered my life, it could not steal my strength.

When I began Adventure Therapy Foundation, I knew I would give all my time and efforts, but I also knew without a goal to use as a focal point, I could give my every effort but find myself moving in a circle. I did not want to waste my time, so I found mentors and set goals to ensure my work took me forward.

I have a sense of urgency in my life. I do not want to waste my energy, emotion, and time on tasks that will not accomplish any purpose. I chose to step back from responsibilities because no matter how much effort I gave, the result would not change. These responsibilities were good choices in my life. I began them because I wanted to help and make a difference. My desire to help and make a difference can draw me toward any number of opportunities. In order to know where to invest my life, I ask myself the question: Is this a good choice or is it a great one? Time is a limited resource. I do not have enough to give my life away to every good option that might present itself. I have a goal—a purpose. If I choose to give my time away to one hundred different good tasks, I will be splintered, stressed, and drained. When I look at my world, I see places that could benefit from my participation. In my mind, I repeat: Stay on course. Stay on course. There are some things only I can do. No one else can step into specific roles, only me. When I invest myself in purposeful tasks and don't protect my time, not only is my identity stolen, but my impact is also erased.

exploring the seasons of emotional healing

Have you ever....

Have you ever worked hard at something but felt you were not getting anywhere? Did you stop to ask yourself why? Why is it difficult to make progress in this area?

Conversely, were there times when you pointed yourself toward a purpose and found yourself moving forward with ease? Did you stop to ask yourself why?

Reflect on these different seasons of life. What is necessary to keep you going? What makes you choose a different path?

Confidence leads to resilience. Purpose leads to strength. Purpose carries us beyond our natural strengths. When my strength is attached to a purpose beyond myself, I am pulled by that ideal to step beyond my limits and take on greater risks. My confidence in that purpose will lead me to a state of resilience. I am not distracted by other pulls in my life. All my strength is given to one purpose, allowing both my strength and my resilience to compound at a greater rate.

I have just walked you through part of my own life, which was initially designed with eighty years in mind and included all the typical highlight moments of children, a career, and retirement. However, when cancer entered the picture, my model for life needed to shift. In the next section, I propose two possible models for life: a pre-diagnosis model and a post-diagnosis model.

Stages of Life

Age of Becoming
The Age of Becoming makes up our formative years. It is the stage of maturing into the people we will become. These years include our K–12 and college education until we have children or enter a career path.

Age of Responsibility
This stage defines the majority of our lifetime. These are the years we work and/or raise children. This stage is directed by the needs of others or the demands of our careers. During the Age of Responsibilty, decisions are made for the common good (the interest of the career/company or the family) rather than the individual.

Golden Age
During this stage, life opportunities become available to us. We can experience the freedom of our desires, and step into formative visions around identity. For some, this age allows a pursuit of passion projects that were delayed by the Age of Responsibility. These projects could be travel, hobbies, new careers, volunteer work, or similar individually significant commitments. The Golden Age allows us to see the Age of Responsibility from a different perspective. With the daily demanding grind behind us, we can appreciate the beauty and grace of those who labor without rest. The Golden Age allows us to serve in such a way that allows others to accomplish more in life than they would have had the opportunity to do without our help. It offers a lift or a step forward to the next generation.

Age of Legacy

This is the stage of giving back. Whether we have financial gifts, talents, or hard-earned wisdom, the Age of Legacy is a voluntary return to help those who are becoming or who work for the common good. During this age, we prioritize the ability to remain available to others. We can choose whom we will support and when. It contrasts with the Age of Responsibility, where a family depends on our work and service. In the Age of Legacy, we can provide relief, guidance, mentoring, training, advice, comfort, support, and financial assistance to others, especially individuals working through the Age of Responsibility or Age of Becoming.

Timeline Model: Future Reward System

A Future Reward System life structure is designed to maximize financial security. It is driven by a proper and safe retirement provided by years of service invested in a career. This timeline is a Future Reward System. For example, the Golden Age occurs after our children exit college and we earn a retirement. It is defined by milestone moments like having a retirement party, attending a child's wedding, or becoming a grandparent. These future rewards symbolize a life well spent. These symbols are more valuable on this timeline than the amount of time they fill. Though a golden moment may only last one day, it holds the significance of all the years prior that led to the celebration. Thus, the reward for a lifetime of responsibility is experienced by a singular party or celebration. Following the celebration, acknowledging the transition from the Age of Responsibility to the Golden Age, a person is expected to begin to experience desires that have been denied or delayed.

The Age of Responsibility requires the delay of many desirable moments. Therefore, in this model, the Golden Age often fills the remainder of one's life. These moments can extend the Golden Age and consume the rest of one's lifetime. The years within the Age of Responsibility can also drain one of health and vitality if a person does not balance the level of responsibility carried over such an extended portion of life. This can diminish the timeline of one's life, eliminating the opportunity to live in the Age of Legacy.

Golden Age Dominant Model

Cancer disrupts the Future Reward System life structure found in a traditional timeline. Post-diagnosis, this system is no longer an acceptable structure for life. An alternative timeline must be created to prioritize health and well-being. This system embraces multiple stages of life at once. The Golden Age is interwoven into many aspects of daily life. While celebration around retirement or a child's wedding remains desirable, experiencing meaning and affirmation is prioritized at a higher rate during daily life. Similarly, the prioritization of familial relationships and celebration of smaller milestones become an acceptable replacement for acknowledging life's rewards.

Cancer offers a time of reflection that allows us to choose how we want to frame our future. The Golden and Legacy Ages are often found to be too important to delay any longer. The skills and talents acquired until this point in life are suddenly combined with the values that would have otherwise been pushed off until later, during the Golden Age. The possibility of living an alternative timeline of passion projects and purpose during the age that would have been the Age of Responsibility becomes possible today. Delaying such

exploring the seasons of emotional healing

desires no longer feels like an option because of the uncertainty of cancer's future impact on the timeline. The alternative timeline requires the Golden Age and Age of Legacy to coexist with the Age of Responsibility.

Pre-Cancer Expectations
FUTURE REWARD SYSTEM MODEL

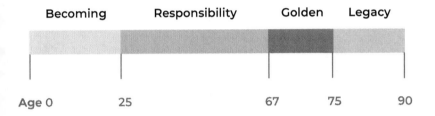

Post-Cancer Expectations
GOLDEN AGE DOMINANT MODEL

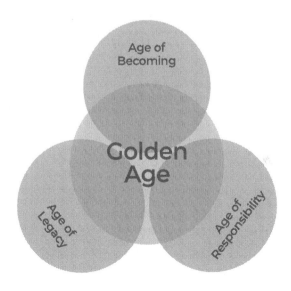

Mourning a Broken Identity

A pre-cancer identity is created in a state of innocence. It involves anticipated twenty-fifth-anniversary trips to Hawaii, fiftieth-anniversary celebrations in Napa, retirement plans that include funds for our children's college tuition, and weddings. These expected milestones can define our identity. Our lives are spent working toward such golden moments. A pre-cancer identity is an untested identity, satisfied with a series of responsibilities that will carry us forward into a "good life."

A cancer diagnosis is an earthquake shaking these expectations for the future. After a cancer diagnosis, twenty years no longer feels like a guarantee. Therefore, life's great moments cannot hang in that distant future. Spending decades investing in a future reward suddenly feels meaningless. A mindset shift must occur to make sense of life itself. An identity based on our expectation of future rewards is lost.

This perspective shift is painful. Our culture and prior expectations have trained us to pursue a golden future. This treasure at the end of a rainbow directed our time. So much of life has been an investment in, one day, finding that treasure. Then when we transition away from a future-reward-identity mindset, we grieve. Whether we knew it or not, those expectations became part of our identity, and now a part of our identity has been lost.

Whenever a piece of our identity is lost, grief is the natural response. If we were once the financial provider for our family and then we were diagnosed with cancer, the time-lapse in our career shatters the certainty of future paychecks. If cancer stalled our job once, it might happen again. The expectations for a steady income and a promising career were a part of our identity. A cancer diagnosis causes us to question these expectations, thus questioning our identity.

For example, the identity of an athlete can be lost as cancer sets aside their strength for a year or more. The hole left in their time, relationships, and entertainment because of the inability to engage in athletic events causes hopelessness and resignation. There is an awareness that the hobbies and friendships attached to those hobbies are something that can be lost. When we lose a piece of our identity, the grief is real. Pieces of our identity will be compromised or broken through our cancer experience.

I struggle with the loss of my independence. When I have a reoccurrence, suddenly, my schedule is not my own. I am at the mercy of a doctor's schedule, a tech's willingness to call me back, or how a scheduler's mood impacts her ability to be flexible around my requests. I can become overwhelmed by a receptionist who does not listen to my needs and get angry when I am treated as one of the thousands of patients who come and go from the clinic. When someone in the office won't learn my name or release my reports, I can carry anger for days. I feel trapped inside a system that I cannot control.

After my initial response of anger, frustration, and hurt, I then stop looking at everyone at the clinic and begin to look at myself. What am I truly experiencing? I am feeling a loss of independence. I must submit control over my own life to people I do not know. I do not know how much of my independence I will need to release. I am afraid of the reoccurrence. I am concerned about the new treatment plan. My identity is threatened.

We each experience grief over the loss of a dream or the loss of certainty. Our worldview has been shaken and shattered. The days of innocence are lost. Grief is then a necessary process.

Whether we want to admit it or not, we are changed by cancer. Most of us cannot honestly return to the person we once were. The good news is that most of us arrived at that former identity by accident. In our twenties, when we began making major life decisions, we weren't what I would call experts. We did our best with where we were, but, hopefully, our post-cancer selves will be a little more informed.

Cancer provides us with a reboot button. Whether cancer finds us in our 30s, 40s, 50s, or 60s, it provides us with a clean slate, an opportunity to reconsider our life's trajectory. I have never met anyone who experienced cancer and, after treatment, wanted to return to their exact life, just as it was. There is a deepened desire to prioritize family, relationships, self-care, purpose, and well-being. We value these things, but often they are set to the side during the Age of Responsibility. We put them to the side, intending to make them the priority in the Golden Age, but not right now.

Cancer reminds us that life's Golden Age must be found where we are today. It brings our values into laser focus. As we face our mortality, we get a clear picture of what is at risk without intentional living.

When our identity is shaken, we discover the value of today. The people we are with and how our lives impact today's world hold deep significance. Cancer causes a perspective shift creating an urgency to live our values in the present rather than waiting to experience some idealistic milestone in the future.

How we engage with our values changes during this shift. Our values must be experienced daily—not the results of the values, but the purposes and values themselves. The decades we spend raising children or paying off mortgages must be meaningful on their own, without a future reward to motivate us. A post-diagnosis identity requires daily purpose.

Values vs. Expectations

Why does every mother want to be present at her daughter's wedding? Is it to see the dress and taste the food? Probably not.

The realization of attending a daughter's wedding has nothing to do with the event itself. My desire to participate in my daughter's wedding has everything to do with being at her side as she faces the highs and lows of life. I want to be present through the process that brought her to this meaningful moment. If you offered me the guarantee that I would be present in every high and low of my daughter's life, but I would not taste her wedding feast or see her dress, I would take that guarantee without hesitation. My heart wants to see her happily creating a life of her own.

Our hearts have deeper desires than experiencing one-time events; they desire to participate in the beauty of life with those we love. Though this is true, we spend many years waiting for an event to confirm we are on the right track. What if today, and every day, we could value the process of life, treasuring the simple moments where our purpose is actualized?

When we embrace the truth that golden moments exist in the present, we are able to acknowledge the heart of our dreams. A mother who holds space for a daughter's highs and lows on any given Wednesday after school is participating in the highs and lows of her life.

Golden moments are available to us today. The experience of cancer shifts our perspective so we may capture thousands of meaningful moments rather than invest all the emotion and purpose of life into one day in the distant future.

Take Every Thought Captive

We are excellent at filtering information; we have to be. There is so much information in the world that we must choose what we listen to and what we don't. Though we have this capability when it comes to information and media, we rarely apply it to our own thoughts.

Taking every thought captive is a tool for recognizing what story is playing in our minds and discerning if this story benefits us.

I had to take every thought captive when I was diagnosed with metastatic breast cancer. I had seemingly infinite scenarios playing out in my mind that all led to my death. Stories of how I would die and how my family would respond filled my days. I was trapped inside a mental framework based on nothing but my own fears. Not one of those stories I walked out in my mind showed me where I am today. None of them explored what I would do with years of remission or how I would find purpose in the pain.

For a period of time, I allowed my thoughts full control of my emotions and time. Whatever fear-based, uncertain thought wanted to pop up, I gave it full power over me. The longer I allowed this to continue, the stronger and truer the thoughts felt. One day I could take it no longer. I felt compelled to make a change in my thoughts. I had to take hold of everything that was not beneficial to me and flag them in my mind as fake news. There is no truth in the certainty of my early death. There is no truth that all of my life was in the past. There was no purpose in living a life defined by fear. I declared these pieces of fake news could no longer dominate my life.

The problem was I did not know what would become of my life. In this uncertainty, I knew there was no benefit in betting on the worst-case scenarios. If I did not know what the future would hold, why not begin writing headlines about my life that represented the person I wanted to be? Why not use the same amount of energy dreaming of cures, success, and an enduring legacy? I worked to take every thought captive. If my thoughts did not align with my values, I blocked them and replaced them with a new story.

Where we direct our thoughts, our actions will follow. I do not know if I saved my own life that day, but I stopped obsessing over death. By choosing to focus on my terminal diagnosis, I was releasing stress hormones into my body twenty-four hours a day. When I began focusing on possibilities, I chose to replace fear with irrational optimism, and my thoughts triggered the release of healing chemicals in my body. Our thoughts matter. They do more than shift our mood, they release possibility over our lives.

Let's consider a scenario. A new promotion opens up at work. This shift in opportunity creates space for many thoughts to emerge: "I am not ready." "Joe is definitely going to get it." "It will be a lot more money but a lot more responsibility." "I don't want to leave my buddies behind." "I would probably not get chosen."

On and on these scenarios play out. We allow our brains to say whatever they want to say, and when we go into the interview, we are already convinced of the outcome. Additionally, when we go into the interview, there are typically more scenarios in our minds stacked against us than for us! Whichever side wins in our minds might just play out in our realities because we demonstrate what we choose to believe. We will either go into the interview confident that our skills and resume prove our value, or we will go into the interview questioning ourselves even before the questions begin.

Unfortunately, most of our thoughts are not based on facts or even truth. Additionally, without discipline, most do not come from our values or purpose either. Taking every thought captive means that when stories emerge in our thoughts, we notice what they are saying, and we choose which of our own ideas will direct our lives.

 Take Action

Select an area in which you hope to undergo personal growth. Write it down and write the reason you want to grow. Why is this area important to you?

For one week, take a moment to write down every thought you have around that area. Any time a thought emerges on that topic, take hold of it. In your mind, grasp that thought and hold it, look at it, and see what is happening. What does that thought sound like? Does it sound like you or someone else you know? Is it making you stronger? If you develop the thought and take it to its greatest potential, will it make you the person you want to be?

If the answer is yes, create space in your mind for that thought to live and grow. If the answer is no, throw the thought away. Get rid of it! Take those pages you have written and rip them up.

The stories you tell yourself can be mental habits. They may not be easily broken. Some thoughts will quickly attempt to return to the front of your mind.

Return to the page where you wrote down why this is important to you. Is this "why" worth fighting for? If so, invest time in letting this thought grow. Be intentional in creating a new narrative in your thoughts. Write a new story for your life. This story will begin as a seed in your thoughts and then will grow into words, actions, and decisions. Now define the growth you seek and begin exploring the outcomes available to you in this new mental space. What possibilities are available to you in your new narrative?

Whenever you find your mind wandering into old habits, take those thoughts captive and release the new narrative. Over time, the new story will become more real to you than the old ones.

REFLECTIONS

Living with Purpose

I live and breathe vision-driven thoughts. I am convinced that my nonprofit will be fully funded any day now, and I will have created a structure of thought that changes the experience of cancer. I have told myself this and acted on it for so long that no other reality feels true. It does not matter whether I ever see the impact of my visionary leadership changing the experience of cancer or not, I am living with purpose. I wake up motivated by the critical work that must be done. I see the problem with the current cancer experience and seek out solutions. Whether or not I reach my goal of changing the cancer experience globally, my belief will change the understanding of cancer at least in every person I encounter.

My days of living out this vision have accumulated into years, and I have spent these years in the exciting pursuit of purpose.

My belief in what is possible opens opportunities for me that I am not even pursuing. They enrich my life and the lives of my family. I do not allow the question "What if my cancer spreads?"

I do not complain about the problems of the world. I am engaged. I am empowered. I am living a purpose-focused life.

If I did not believe in the future existence of these things, there would be no chance of changing the cancer experience. I would be bored, spend too much money, and overeat chocolate, cheese, and bread—discontent and unengaged.

> **Understanding my personal purpose gives me strength that rises above every circumstance.**

Instead, I am activated. I know what I want to do, believe I can do it, and invest my time and talents into that mission. Though I am still far from achieving my goals, I feel myself drawing closer every day.

This is my life, shaped by a post-cancer, Golden Age dominant worldview. I embrace my Age of Legacy, Age of Responsibility, and Golden Ages of life all at once. Every moment is abundant. Every day matters.

PART 1 CONCLUSION:

A TYPICAL EMOTIONAL RESPONSE TO CANCER

building language that defines the emotional impact of cancer acknowledges the person impacted by a disease. Words like patient and survivor are based on a person's relationship to a disease and its treatment. In that context, there is no room for a person or their emotions. By defining the emotional side effects of cancer, we begin to build a framework that allows the whole person to be acknowledged. This holistic approach allows all of us to understand the true impact of cancer better.

Fear, isolation, and a broken identity are typical responses to cancer. They are typical, meaning these experiences are normal, common, and classic. However, their presence in the life of a person impacted by cancer has never been acknowledged. Since it has been overlooked for decades, those impacted by these emotional side effects also feel unseen. When treatments end and early survivorship begins, we expect a full and hasty recovery. So when we find a terrible emotional burden waiting for us, we feel embarrassed and ashamed of its presence. We expect to begin to recover and instead find ourselves only beginning to process the grief and pain caused by the trauma of cancer. This is a difficult disappointment, and when we become overwhelmed by these burdens, we do not know where to turn.

Without an expectation of the need for emotional recovery, the presence of fear, isolation, and brokenness in an early survivor can become a source of shame, compounded isolation, and multiplied fear. Furthermore, without a proper context of the healing process, the trauma of cancer can be construed as permanent emotional damage. Conversely, by defining the emotional experience of cancer, we can begin to understand our own story. Our emotional burdens do not need to remain hidden or ignored because this common language allows us to have authentic conversations and begin to feel acknowledged.

Now, when a person completes treatment, she will know to expect that a season of emotional healing is required. This expectation eliminates the shock and embarrassment of grief. Families can foresee the need for emotional recovery from cancer. Those impacted by cancer can speak honestly about how they are recovering. Because of this common knowledge, families can support one another despite their shared grief. This shift in expectations around the experience of cancer will minimize the emotional impact of cancer and expedite a full recovery from the disease. This is why it is imperative that we better understand the emotional experience of the trauma of cancer.

Part 2
The Healing Process

Tree Rings

I grew up in the woods. Tennessee is nothing but green, and you can find woods anywhere. I love trees—the smell, the way the light shines through the leaves, and the sound of the wind moving through the forest. When I moved to California, I missed the presence of trees. Of course, there are plenty of decorative trees, but I missed the relationship one tree has with the next and the way trees grow together in a forest. To get my tree fix, I started traveling to spaces where I could find old-growth forests in California, and that led me to the love of redwoods.

Redwood trees are some of the earth's oldest, largest, and most resilient living things. Yet these trees come from one of the smallest seeds of any tree. Redwoods grow interconnected; their roots link, share resources, and strengthen one another. From this linking of roots, they can sustain their strength in times of fire or drought. Because of their grove, they can grow to great heights.

The symbol of tree rings is a reminder that growth is constantly occurring. Each ring in a tree represents one year of growth. The rings tell the story of what type of year the tree experienced. If resources were abundant, the ring would be thicker. The rings can

> "While it feels safer for many of us to hide our painful stories, redwoods carry their scars on the outside throughout their one thousand years of life."

also demonstrate the stresses a tree endured, such as fire, drought, or other hardships. If it was a difficult year, the rings would be closer together.

Redwood trees need difficulties to survive. In fact, fire is necessary for the release of redwood seeds. It is only through hardship that a new generation of redwood seedlings will grow. It is through the heat of the fire that the redwood's tiny cones become dry enough to release the seeds. The fire also burns away any brush that might suffocate the seedling. So beyond releasing the seeds, the fire creates space for the seeds to take root. This process allows the tiniest of seeds to take their place among the great tree giants that will soon support them.

When visiting a redwood grove, you can see evidence of their difficult pasts. Walking among redwoods, you can witness the bulges on the sides of their massive trunks. These "burls" are formed as a last-ditch effort to save the tree's life after an injury or infection. A burl protects a tree like a scar. Redwoods use burls for self-defense, but the burls can also sprout and create new redwood trees.

These scars create a visible story of the trials the trees have faced, and we can witness that out of these scars, new life grows.

While it feels safer for many of us to hide our painful stories, redwoods carry their scars on the outside throughout their one thousand years of life. Their wounds did not kill them, and the scars did not diminish their beauty. Instead, their scars created an opportunity for them to sprout other young trees. The weakness of one tree becomes the strength of the next.

If you need encouragement or feel as if you are the only one wearing the scars from life on the outside, take a walk in the woods. The woods offer reassurance that no matter what season we find ourselves in, beauty abounds.

> " The weakness of one tree becomes the strength of the next. "

THE HEALING PROCESS

the emotional experience of cancer has never been defined. A problem that has never been defined cannot be resolved. To truly understand cancer, we must understand every way it impacts a life. We have gone to great lengths to become aware of the physical impact of cancer. Conversely, we have yet to begin defining its emotional impact. If we desire to minimize the true impact of cancer, we must establish tools that minimize the long-term emotional damage cancer causes. If we can define the typical emotional side effects of cancer, we can also create systems that allow a person to heal emotionally from the trauma of cancer.

To understand the true impact of cancer, we must first clarify the difference between being cured and being healed. A cure ensures no further damage will be done to your body. A cure is what research creates and what a pink ribbon represents. A cure is what we think we want. Healing, on the other hand, reverses the damage, brokenness, and scars. Healing is what we need. Healing and a cure are not found on the same path. We may very well find a cure for cancer in the coming years. The question we have failed to ask is once a cure is found, will the millions impacted by cancer instantaneously be healed? Additionally, will the children of these cancer survivors, their loved ones, and spouses also be completely relieved of their emotional trauma? Absolutely not.

A cure is necessary to stop the cycle of destruction cancer creates, but only healing will ensure the emotional impact of cancer does not continue to haunt us for generations. The legacy of today's cancer will be found in the emotional, relational, spiritual, and mental health of this generation, as well as the next. Even when a cure is found, and cancer is no longer a threat to our physical well-being, the impact of cancer will continue. For generations, there will be a need to pursue healing to address the emotional side effects of cancer.

We must know the difference between discovering a cure and prioritizing healing. Without a doubt, we must pursue both. As we consider this, it is important to acknowledge the scope of each. To provide a cure, we look only at those who have received a diagnosis. When each person with a cancer diagnosis is cured, we know we have been successful. On the other hand, the emotional impact of cancer is contagious. Those impacted by the emotional side effects of cancer are far greater than those impacted physically. When a loved one is diagnosed with cancer, those who love that person experience fear, isolation, and broken dreams. They become co-survivors of cancer. To think that cancer only impacts a patient is to misunderstand the cancer experience. Fear, isolation, and broken dreams are the lessons cancer teaches our children, co-survivors, and loved ones. Therefore, tools for healing are needed by many more than those with a cancer diagnosis. Even if cancer will no longer be a terminal illness in the next thirty years, the emotional side effects of cancer will be an ever-present burden unless we begin to address these needs today.

exploring the seasons of emotional healing

While many resources are put toward pursuing a cure, there is an ever-growing need for resources that will create tools to help everyone impacted by cancer achieve healing.

When we think of "beating cancer," we often think about ringing the bell on the last day of treatment. Ringing the bell creates a sense of completion. However, the year after cancer treatments can be just as difficult and complex as the treatment process. It isn't until treatments end that our physical and emotional healing can begin.

Understanding physical health is second nature because we have been trained since childhood in how to help our bodies heal. Acknowledging physical pain is socially acceptable, and responding to physical illness with rest and hydration is second nature. Yet, how do we heal our emotional selves? When we are hurt emotionally or experience emotional trauma, what process do we use to ensure healing and recovery? Are there steps we should take to acknowledge emotional trauma? Do we confess this pain exists and let others know we are in a season of rest and recovery? There is significantly less clarity around emotional health than physical health.

When we have a physical wound, there is an understood rhythm:

1. When there is a trauma that causes an injury, this trauma is stopped as quickly as possible to prevent further pain.
2. Bleeding and cleansing take place to clear away any toxin or foreign substance that needs to be removed to clearly view the wound and promote healing.
3. A scab covers the wound and provides a thin layer of protection.
4. The growth of the new skin occurs.
5. The healing process is complete.

In this book, I want to propose a similar process for responding to emotional traumas like cancer. Some of this process occurs whether or not we are consciously pursuing emotional healing. Just as our bodies will bleed, create a scab, and regrow new skin without our intervention, some of the emotional healing will happen whether we take intentional steps or not. However, especially when it comes to deeper traumas than the daily emotional scrape, steps need to be taken to ensure we do not continue to live in pain. If I were to break my arm and did not see a doctor, my arm would eventually heal on its own, probably not the way I would want it to heal, though. Without the protection and support of a cast, I would live in daily pain as the bone moved around on its own. Healing might come over time, but not quickly and not without significant daily frustration and pain. When we do not acknowledge our emotional traumas, it is as if we have a broken arm and are not allowing it to be protected and supported by a cast. Pain remains much longer than necessary. Then, when we heal, we may not heal quite the way we could have if we had taken the time to intentionally care for the emotional wounds.

In my mind, emotional traumas are like a fire. It begins with an unexpected spark and quickly causes a person to run away from its threat as quickly as possible. Like a fire, the initial need is to put as much space between ourselves and the threat of harm. A fire then destroys everything in its path. It does not discern between what is valuable and what is trivial. It destroys everything it touches until it runs out of fuel. Once subsided, a fire leaves nothing but a void filled with ash. What comes next is up to us. We can re-create a life from the ash, or we can walk away. One way or another, we must grow from the trauma. Grow a new life, with new expectations, until one day we find life is restored.

This is how the emotional trauma of cancer feels to me. A fire ravaged my life. I was left with nothing but a blank slate and the values and purposes that were found at my core. These values and purposes are like seeds, buried deep within me, so deep that not even the traumatic fire of metastatic cancer can scorch them.

From this metaphor, I propose the seasons of emotional healing:

1. **Fire:** This is the season of trauma. Nothing can be done except to act, however possible, to minimize the damage and pain. Fire represents how life feels when a threat exists. In the experience of cancer, this is where our emotions remain until treatment ends.

2. **Void:** The trauma is over, but we must observe the damage done. Often, this is the first time we see what has been lost. This season requires a detailed look at not only what was lost, but also what remains. It represents the first year after treatment or early-survivorship.

3. **Growth:** Decisions are made during this season on how to move forward, and the first steps are taken on a new path.

4. **Restoration:** Life is built and rebuilt until the new path feels true to who we are today.

5. **Giving:** Once we are no longer in pain and begin to feel strong in our newly regrown life, a natural response is to see the lives of others differently. Trauma exponentially multiplies empathy, and in this season, you can choose to use your restored strength to support others.

The Seasons of Healing

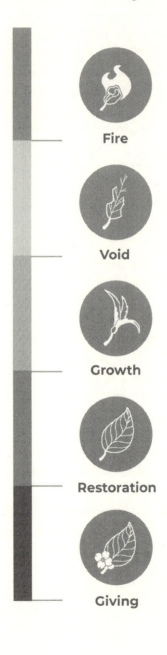

These physical and emotional healing processes parallel one another. During the physical healing process, we can observe daily changes in the wound. The emotional healing process is much more challenging to observe, so we must pay closer attention. When we pay attention, we can observe slow changes happening in our emotional state just as a physical wound might change from day to day. Our emotional healing process takes significantly longer to recover than a small cut, but just as the body wants to heal, so do our true selves.

The healing process is as much for others as it is for us. Those who surround us become co-survivors in our cancer journeys. While the trauma is happening to us, those who love us must sit on the sidelines, observing our pain. They may not understand it right away, but they too are being changed by our disease. Once we escape the fire of our traumas, others might assume the experience of cancer has come to an end. The emotional healing process is nearly impossible for others to observe with clarity, so it is imperative for us to have the words to communicate where we are in the stages of emotional healing. Only then can others know how to support us.

It is only when others are taught to observe our emotional healing process that they can find the assurance that we are well. When we don't have the words or tools to achieve emotional healing, those who love us remain unsettled and on alert for our sake longer than necessary. Their uncertainty around our well-being feeds our fears, causing us to stay in the trauma of cancer much longer than is needed. Conversely, they may choose to believe no further trauma is present. They may push us to return to our "old selves" which can feel insulting to the healing process. The lack of understanding around the emotional healing process can create uncertainty in our loved ones and can become a barrier to our relationships with them.

The identity of someone who has been impacted by cancer shifts throughout the cancer experience; it is unavoidable. Those living with us might sense this shift yet lack clarity around what is happening inside of us. Just as we, patients and survivors, must do the work of moving through treatments, we must also choose to walk through the process of emotional restoration. We must do the work of pursuing emotional healing for our own sake and for the sake of those we love. It is only by continuing to pursue emotional healing that survivors and our families, or co-survivors, will become stronger because of the impact of cancer.

This book is written to help you find the language to clarify the restoration process. Without words around this experience, your loved ones will not understand your heart or path forward. This book is my attempt at supporting you and those you love the most. Communication in this season of healing will help your relationships remain strong and in alignment despite all the changes that might occur inside of you.

The second section of this book attempts to provide words that describe the experience of cancer and the emotional healing process. These metaphors and personal reflections are designed to help you articulate your experiences and needs as you walk through the healing process.

CHAPTER 4

Fire

Living in California has taught me a lot about wildfires. Wildfires are hard to fathom. How can a fire spread at forty miles per hour? It moves so fast that the fire can overtake a car driving away. In five seconds, everything you see will disappear and be gone forever. It is challenging to comprehend heat so intense it consumes everything in its path. In California, there are entire mountains left in a state of blank nothingness after a fire passes through. I have witnessed mountains where one side of the road is charred, and the other is lush and green. As I pass through, I recognize the thin line between life and death. To the left of me, I witness beautifully abundant life, and to the right, darkness and loss—a place where only the shadows of life remain.

A cancer diagnosis holds the same intensity. Sparks fly out of the words "you have cancer," and a thin line is created. These three words create a line that signifies the before and after. Before cancer was a time of innocence, laughter, and beauty. It was a time when plans for twenty years into the future were commonplace and growing old felt like a hardship. After cancer is a space where every plan, expectation, and dream begins to whither. After cancer, the future is uncertain, and every personal strength comes into question. For a new patient, a cancer diagnosis and its treatments are like fleeing from a fire. There is no time to pause and take inventory of what will be left behind. There is only an urgency to act and preserve life. Pushing forward is exhausting and full of uncertainty and fear. It leaves us bankrupt of emotional and physical strength. However difficult, the threat of cancer requires an immediate response, a decision to fight through the unknowns ahead in hopes that we might escape its threat.

During the early days of my metastatic diagnosis, I felt as if cancer and my ultimate death was present, constantly surrounding me. No one could step into the fire of my life and offer an escape. No words of comfort could rescue me from the situation. When my doctor told us not to worry about prognosis or a timeline, the words sounded like she had no hope to offer. My cancer had grown despite the two years of the harshest treatment. What hope could there be? Everywhere I looked, death and darkness circled me.

During this time, when others asked me how they could help, I asked them to love my girls. I had come to understand that eventually my love would not be present for them, and others would need to step into the emptiness of where I should be. Every decision was tainted by darkness. I was running from death, yet there was no escape. Death was circling and enveloping me. It didn't matter if I was making decisions for next week or next month or next year, the questions were: Will it matter? Will I be here? Who can carry this out if I am gone? The questions of uncertainty filled my mind so completely, not much else could exist. My life was burning, not the stuff that surrounded my life, but my life itself was being scorched.

When mountains are on fire, you can smell the smoke from hundreds of miles away. It fills the air and erases the horizon. Ash falls from the sky, coating the world in grey.

When given a cancer diagnosis, your dreams are fluttering in the air. Broken remnants of what was, fall from the sky, creating layers of greyness that hold grief and disappointment. While those untouched by cancer effortlessly plan family vacations, purchase new cars, or make home improvements, new patients sit in the thick smoke of their own lives, wondering how they might ever enter that world of simplicity again.

I remember a moment when I felt my life had been reduced to breathing in and out and pondered the question of how many more moments I would get to experience breath. I sat in a room while others discussed cruise ships and the colors they wanted to paint their walls. It felt like our worlds were a universe apart. I sat on one side of the fire line covered in ash, and they were safely cultivating the endless opportunities located on the other side of the fire line.

When you first receive a cancer diagnosis, your mind fills with "smoke." Everything feels like it is working together to choke you. It is hard to live among those who are not fleeing for their own life. It is difficult to see life as others see it. It is nearly impossible to engage in conversation or interaction that doesn't fill you with uncertainty.

Just as escaping a fire happens only for a quick, dramatic moment, this initial response to a cancer diagnosis only lasts for a season. The harshness of the moment cannot be overlooked, but on the road ahead, there is hope.

The Diagnosis

The words "you have cancer" are like the tiniest spark released in a dry forest. It starts small and unexpectedly, but the impact is unimaginable. After these words are spoken, there is only one priority: survival. You must do whatever it takes to survive. This means jobs, responsibilities, vacations, plans, and relationships are all secondary to the singular goal of escape. You must escape the threat of cancer, the side effects of treatment, and the mental burden of your shifting life. Unlike running from a wildfire, escaping cancer is not a one-time experience but a cycle. First, you must learn to outrun the fear of the words spoken at diagnosis. Then, you must outrun the fear of the treatments. Fear swirls around the idea of cancer, its treatments, the side effects of those treatments, the scans, and the changes in relationships. This swirling fear allows you to escape for a moment or two from one wave of change, but as soon as you get your feet under you, the next wave hits. Each spark that lands in your life requires that you shift your course, your expectations, and your priorities.

The diagnosis season is overwhelming. However, during these moments, there are many people providing you with direction. Nurses, doctors, treatment schedules, and hopefully, a few new cancer friends are present to help you formulate a plan. Though the support feels minimal compared to the weight of change occurring, these systems and kind faces move you forward. They are pointing you in the right direction, answering questions, and will be at your side during this first season. Though many appointments and texts might feel overwhelming, their presence provides assurance. You have a plan. You are taking action against the threat. You are doing all that can be done.

During the first months of diagnosis, these life adjustments fill your mind. It is important to remember, at this time, you are not an expert at coping with the cancer experience. You do not know the best way forward and do not even know what questions to ask to find the best way forward. There will be time down the road to learn, adapt, and grow, but in this moment, there is only time to respond. Allow yourself the freedom to be innocent and even ignorant. Cancer is a complicated disease, and despite decades of research, researchers still don't know what they don't know. You may look back on these first few months and wish you had taken a different path. That is OK. Everything you know about cancer in the future will be because of these initial moments. This is the spark, the beginning, and you have the rest of your life to allow this spark to shape the path before you.

Strength

Before diagnosis, you were probably like many others, physical strength was something you took for granted. Every day you counted your steps, aiming to walk ten thousand. These steps were used to buy groceries, run the carpool, go to work, and perhaps hit the gym. Every step had a goal of moving physically and emotionally toward a healthy life. When treatments begin, you must learn to redefine your strength. During chemo, you learn to count your steps, except with the opposite intention. While receiving treatments, you may only have the strength to walk three thousand steps daily. Pre-treatment, you were prompted to jump out of your chair to get your blood pumping every hour. During chemo, the goal becomes remaining on the couch to save up every step available to you. It feels very counter-cultural, almost wrong to rest and rest, and then rest some more.

Early cancer treatments introduce you to the experience of feeling limited. The limitation of strength in this season is the first opportunity you have to witness your deeper priorities. When your strength begins to fail, it is important to notice a few things. First, how do you use the strength you have? If you only have three thousand steps of strength a day, where are your feet taking you?

When I was in chemo, I tried very hard to remain still during the day when my girls were at school and my husband was at work. This allowed me to engage and participate in the evening when my family was together. Where I used my limited energy revealed how much I valued family time. When I had unlimited strength and energy, I may not have consciously recognized that the few hours of family time each night was the most important part of my day.

When you have no physical strength, emotionally it feels like a lack of control. Without strength, you cannot fix social situations, physical circumstances, or even dinner. So the second thing you begin to observe about yourself is which situations unsettle you. What is the number one thing you want to fix as soon as you find your strength? What is rolling over and over in your head as you lay on the couch? What situation makes you feel like you have lost control of your life? It is important to write down the aspects of life that leave you unsettled during treatments. These points of control reveal a lot about who you are and what values drive your life. The better you understand these trigger points in your life now, the easier it will be to understand yourself as you rebuild your identity in the future.

Take Action

Consider where you choose to use your energy and where you feel out of control due to a lack of strength. Write these down.

The places you invest the limited energy you have are tied to your deepest values. Dig deeper into those values. What do they feel like? Are they relational or goal-oriented? If you lose more energy, how will these values shift? Even if you become very weak, can you preserve these values?

Now consider the areas of life that drive you crazy, those spaces you cannot change because of your limitations. What makes those spaces so important? What ideas do you hold about how those spaces should be? What expectations do you have for yourself and others in these areas? Can you imagine those spaces any other way? What resources do you have to help you in these areas?

Limitations can reveal your strengths. They can teach you what you desire and help you begin to use parts of yourself that you have never acknowledged before. Remember, your physical strength is only one of the strengths you possess. As you adjust to limited physical strength while in treatment, discover the multitude of other strengths you have to offer. Explore who you could become if your strengths were utilized more.

REFLECTIONS

The Unexpected Diagnosis

When I was diagnosed with stage three cancer, there was an urgency to get me into treatment. On the day of my initial scans, my doctor stayed in her office until 7:00 p.m. Her urgency told me every moment mattered. Within days of being told I had cancer, I was scheduled for port surgery, and then I immediately started chemo. I continued down this urgent path for almost a year. I hadn't been cleared to drive after my double mastectomy, yet I was asked to find a way to come into the cancer center every day for radiation.

For a year and a half, I had more than eight surgeries, chemo, and radiation. During that time, my thoughts moved from one treatment to the next. There was no room for any thoughts except moving forward. I didn't question the system. I was thrown into a system I knew nothing of. I asked questions but understood very few of the decision points. I knew so little; I don't think it was possible to ask a question that might have changed my path. There was a system for my cancer, and I was running along the path with doctors in front of me and behind me, each one telling me to move a little faster. The only question I really knew how to ask was where to show up for my next appointment. I remember liking doctors who told me optimistic outcomes and disliking doctors who looked worried. I moved along my treatment path, and the only choice I struggled over was whether I could continue to act strong or break down and cry. I stayed relatively strong during chemo, but once I started radiation, I spent a lot of time crying. Perhaps it was the daily trips to the cancer center, perhaps it was the way I was rushed in and out without any personal interaction, or perhaps it was the pain. Radiation felt like one push too far.

Then one day, I had my last treatment. I am sure someone patted me on the back and sent me on my way, but I don't remember any acknowledgment that day. What I do remember is stepping into the parking lot and thinking, so yesterday I had cancer, and today I don't? The question was unsettling.

> "After cancer, the future is uncertain, and every personal strength comes into question."

REFLECTIONS: A CO-SURVIVOR'S PERSPECTIVE

You Are Strong Enough

I suppose that everybody's first thought when they hear of a cancer diagnosis—whether it be a loved one or their own—is: I never thought that this would happen to me. This thought is persistent. For months after my wife's diagnosis, I would wake up and think, Thank God, it was only a dream! But this fleeting sense of relief was always replaced with the realization that it wasn't just a horrible nightmare. I was really facing a reality in which my wife had received a stage four breast cancer diagnosis. Eventually, the truth sinks in, and you understand and accept that not only can this happen to you, but it did. This is, perhaps, the first step in dealing with the devastating news. Only after you have accepted the harsh reality can you begin to cope with it.

I think that the next step is understanding that this is going to be really, really hard. Cancer is (probably) going to stretch you physically, emotionally, spiritually, and financially to your breaking point. You will face exhaustion, depression, anger, and frustration. Your relationships will be strained (especially with your spouse), and every day will be a battle to stay the course.

The final step, however, in coming to terms with a cancer diagnosis, is to accept, or at least believe, that you are strong enough to do this. You can physically complete all the tasks required of you. Exhaustion may set in, but you can be strong enough to do what it takes. Your emotions are going to be strained to the point of breaking, but you can cope. You know that depression and anger are going to be your daily companions, but you also know that you can master them, or at least hold them at bay. Questions about your faith, your place in the universe, and the lack of justice in the world may

> "
> The questions of uncertainty filled my mind so completely, not much else could exist.
> "

swirl in your mind, but you can (and must!) hold tight to your faith. Hope is your greatest ally. Your finances will be pushed to the limit, but you can and will make it through. Bank accounts may suffer for a moment, but what is lost during treatments can be replaced. Your relationship with your spouse can remain strong even as you both are tested and pushed together. You can come together rather than being forced apart. You can make it through this, and you will.

On this journey there are many who desperately want to help you, and you need their help. When you hear, "What do you need?" Have an answer ready. Don't be afraid to tell them what you need! Maybe you need a sympathetic ear to just listen. Perhaps you need meals delivered because cooking for the kids is too much right now. Maybe you need financial assistance. Ask! They need to help you just as much as you need the help. Do not deprive them of the chance. Let them come alongside you in your times of need, for their sake as well as your own.

-Dr. Clifton Huffmaster

CHAPTER 5

Void

Once the fire has swept across the mountain and run out of fuel, the heat dissipates and the ash settles. It is only after the flames have been subdued that the extent of the damage can be evaluated. After a fire, where a thriving eco-system once existed, now only barrenness can be found. The trees will have burned at differing levels, some completely consumed, and others charred only on the surface, but everything in the path of the fire has been scarred. As you look out over the mountainside, there is an emptiness, a void. An unsettling quietness is felt, defined by much more than the lack of sound. Spires of charred trees stand alone, disconnected on the horizon. The space is now defined by what is no longer present, by the void.

In cancer, Void is the season of transitioning from life as a patient into early survivorship. As a patient, you find all your strength focuses on surviving. The effort of moving through the treatment calendar and recovering between appointments requires all of your mental and physical strength. Then, one day, you ring the bell or get a certificate of completion. Someone declares treatments are over, and you are now "a survivor." You walk out of the door of the cancer center and look at the parking lot and wonder what comes next. This question, this uncertainty of the next step, is the beginning of the Void.

Since the moment you heard the words, "you have cancer," your mind has been in crisis mode. Now, for the first time, you can stop and take inventory of the experience of cancer.

In these first moments, when the role of the patient ends, a new perspective unfolds to reveal how everything in life has shifted and changed. This process is called the Void. The Void is an in-between moment. You are no longer the person you were before cancer, but you have not yet learned who you will be now that life has been impacted by cancer. This can be the most challenging season of the cancer experience.

During treatment, there was a path to walk, a calendar to follow and someone calling from the cancer center to check in. Cancer was manageable because there was a plan. Nurses and techs understood what you were going through. Then one day, no oncology professionals are at your side. You feel alone and without direction. Furthermore, this is the first chance you have had to take inventory of what everyone else was doing during your treatments. As you look around, you learn that friends, activities, and routines from your pre-cancer life are also gone. You stepped out of the stream of life for a year, and your pre-cancer identity moved forward without you. The Void begins here.

The Void is uncomfortable, this can't be understated. It might be the most difficult moment of the cancer experience. It is a time of processing grief. As you take a look at your life, you see that with each missed opportunity, lost relationship, and unobtainable memory, grief is there. During treatment, we grieved the idea of cancer and the physical sacrifices associated with the diagnosis. It is only now that the emotional implications become clear. Each piece of ourselves, the expectations we held, the strengths we thought were unshakable, the ideals we held in our innocence must be grieved. In the Void, the absence of a guarantee around our life expectations becomes very clear. What is gone and what we thought was promised but now feels frail, must all be grieved.

The Void is also an opportunity to begin life again. Routines and responsibilities are minimized or gone. Life has slowed to a halt due to cancer, and in this moment, what is important becomes very clear. The Void provides space for each of us to decide how to begin again. This empty slate can feel overwhelming. It does not feel comfortable. It feels isolating and uncertain, but inside this empty space, there is potential. There is an opportunity to live an intentional, purpose-filled life.

The Void has more potential than any other moment in the cancer experience. However, because it feels uncomfortable in the Void, you may rush through this season. You may want to get out of the emptiness and grief as quickly as possible. Please don't! Think of the Void as a foundation or fertile ground.

I live at the end of a long road. We bought a home there because we are an hour from fantastic opportunities in the San Francisco Bay Area, but our children get to grow up surrounded by cow fields, orchards, and vineyards. We like the balance. After six years of living at the end of the road, others found these undeveloped fields and began dropping subdivision after subdivision all around us. I tell my girls that our town's only hobby is digging in the dirt. We watched subdivisions transition from cow fields into homes. While we drove past these fields, we were constantly surprised that these subdivisions always took longer than expected. At first, bulldozers leveled the ground, and then it seemed like these dirt lots sat and sat and sat. It appeared like nothing was happening at all. In reality, electricity, plumbing, the internet, and even the new homes' foundations were prepared during this seemingly dormant time. Everything that makes a house solid and stable is established in what seems to be a stagnant, inactive season.

The Void is the season of healing that lays a foundation for the future years of life. By not rushing through this season, you prepare a strong foundation in your life. It is a season that lets you process the disappointments and hurt of cancer, so you do not continue to carry your hurt long after the trauma of cancer has ended. Though you may appear dormant to those who pass by, you are healing emotionally and physically. Without a season of healing, you will always have cracks in the foundation of your life.

A common expectation, and likely the experience of most cancer patients, is this idea that once treatment ends, or once a person's hair is growing back, cancer is a thing of the past. No longer is cancer a part of your life, and you are ready to "get back" to who you were. No assumption could be more wrong.

When treatment ends, the most challenging part of cancering begins. It is then, and only then, that you can begin processing what the experience of cancer means to you.

Beginning Again

The Void is a particularly difficult season because during this time you are required to live in two perspectives.

The first paradigm is shaped by your past that includes your former dreams and ideals. Your pre-cancer life shaped your expectations for the future. Your vision of the future was based on the foundation of your past experiences. Your thoughts for the future were based on pre-cancer resources.

exploring the seasons of emotional healing

Looking into the future, you may have counted on things like retirement, golden years, travel with friends and family, and celebrations. These dreams for your future were based on the seemingly guaranteed resources of your life. You spent time and resources in the present building a better future. However, the impact of cancer erases certainty around those ideals.

In this season of healing, letting go of these future golden moments becomes an emotional reality. Here you are, holding in one hand these future dreams, dreams you have spent much of your life investing in, dreams that seemed honorable and worthy of your time. In the Void, you find yourself holding as tightly as possible to this old paradigm while recognizing these expectations may never come to pass. So much of life was invested in an ideal. Retirement, health, financial stability, and travel were the lifelong treasures worth working toward. Suddenly, those expectations come into question. The innocence of certainty is erased. The greatest struggle in this season is letting go of certainty. The ideals you once allowed to define your identity may be available in the future. However, cancer takes away your innocence of believing those ideals are a certainty.

The Void can be the lowest point of your grief. Grief is an emotion felt often in the experience of cancer. Grief is often only discussed around the loss of a loved one, but the emotion of grief is experienced hundreds, if not thousands of times throughout cancer. You grieve over your physical changes, for lost opportunities, for the moments when you can't muster the strength to stand. In the Void, you experience the deepest pains of grief, for you must grieve the life you thought you would live. To be clear, this is not about grieving over an impending death, this is grief around a life that will not unfold as expected. It is grief over the person you wanted to be, for the golden moments of old age that no longer feel guaranteed, and for lost relationships, finances, dreams, and plans. You must acknowledge and grieve the traumatic impact of cancer on your life.

Grief is healthy, it is typical, it is how we ensure our lives don't become swallowed up by the experience of cancer. To grieve is to acknowledge and allow frustration, anger, sadness, disappointment, and every other emotion that fills us to be released. To skip this process is to keep these hurts, to carry them with us into our future. It is normal for patients, survivors, and co-survivors to grieve, but we do not need to feel it forever.

In the Void, we begin a process of self-reflection. We look at what our lives hold, and what our hands hold when it comes to life. If we look into our minds and envision our hands in front of us, one hand clings to the ideals of pre-cancer life, ideals that may not come to be, and the other hand is empty. The second paradigm we must become familiar with during the Void is the feeling of emptiness. Often, after cancer, there is a lack of direction, a loss of purpose and even an emptiness at our core. What we expected and invested in is now filled with uncertainty, so we are filled with new questions: What is certain? What can I invest my life in that cannot be shaken by unforeseen traumatic circumstances, like cancer? What purposes are worthy of my time, money, and talents? How do I want to continue to live?

We must sit in the Void until our questions are truly answered and the struggle to preserve a future that shifted ends. To release an old paradigm does not mean that good things will not exist in our future. There is goodness and even greatness on the horizon. However, we will never fully experience what is available to us if we use all of our energy fighting to hold onto something that no longer exists. We might want to chase the mirage of our former dreams, but if we remain in denial, we will not heal. Instead, we must honor what was. By looking at our intentions for the past and the future, we recognize the purpose of our hearts.

Gifts

I am a gift giver. I enjoy finding the perfect gift for someone. I especially appreciate receiving a gift that demonstrates someone's knowledge of me. These gifts demonstrate love. Someone watches you, looking for ways to make you happy or to relieve a hurt. Then the person uses their creativity, time, and money to locate a unique item that fits who you are.

When I think of the Void, I think of myself standing with my palms turned upward. When I look at my hands, one hand is holding tightly to this gift I was preparing for a happy future, the other hand remains empty and still. It is outstretched with nothing to grasp. There is no direction, and no gift has been prepared for a future impacted by cancer.

The plans we make for the future, the plans for family and friends, are the ultimate gift. These plans take a lifetime to curate and obtain. The time and effort invested in making them come to be increases the value of this gift. As we spend our lives saving and working for a golden future, the importance of these gifts is immeasurable.

When our lives are impacted by cancer, that treasured gift is in our hands, half-complete, and in the Void, there is a realization that this masterful demonstration of love may never be completed. It leaves the time and energy invested in the gift feeling empty. So we sit in the Void season, looking at this dream, this gift of life in our hands, a gift that may no longer be given, and we can be overcome with grief.

The Void is a season of disappointment, loss, hurt, and broken expectations. The weight of past expectations and the emptiness of a new paradigm for the future are equal burdens.

It is said that time will heal all hurts, and in some way, this is what must happen. The Void cannot be rushed. We must remain still, holding our past and future, until gazing at these two paradigms no longer fills us with pain. When we can look upon the gift of the past and the uncertainty of the future without pain, only then can we begin the next season of healing.

In the beginning of the Void season, the future we hold in our hands will be frailer than our past dreams. The past was filled with untested theories and unquestionable certainty. Our futures are built by a life tested and refined by fire. The process of building a vision for the future will come slowly. It will come slowly but will carry with it a new gift. Healing will begin as we learn to rest in the middle of uncertainty. When we can embrace the quiet reflections of our hearts and forgive ourselves for what cannot be known, only then are we ready to grow.

Two Types of Dreams: Calling and Casting

Why do we look to the future and place an expectation, a plan, or a dream into that empty space ahead? There is never a guarantee that the open space in life will adequately hold the vision we create; yet despite our fears and anxieties about life, we keep planning.

Dreaming, or planning (for those who prefer practical language) gives our lives a particular trajectory. We cast a vision of our lives, and in it we go to college, get married, have two children, find a job we love, and grow old on a swing hanging from a huge tree in the back yard. This simple visual image is a forty-year dream, defining how we hope our lives will unfold. It is a dream that may or may not occur over an entire lifetime. This dream, and others like it, provides the next forty years with a trajectory. These visions can create our expectations. They remind us of what we want, and then we, through our decisions, attempt to make the vision into a reality. These are casting dreams, or expectations we consciously place on our lives.

There is another type of dream. There are calling dreams inside each of us that don't come from a conscious directive. These dreams are more like puzzle pieces, a shadow of a dream that seems to call us forward in significant moments in our lives. We may not be able to put a name to them or explain the "why," but these pieces remain, and even when ignored, they do not go away. Since this type of dream is foggy and often unclear, it is easy to replace a calling dream with a shinier, more easily planned casting dream. No matter how long we ignore them, these deep identity callings do not fade. These wispy dreams are often overlooked until cancer breaks the glass, protecting our nicely curated vision. When life's path becomes cracked by the impact of cancer, these deeper callings become louder than ever.

The treatments and recovery of cancer wipe out all of our busyness. They erase so many forty-year plans, bringing us into the present moment. The experience of cancer makes us come to the questions: Who am I today? What is important today? What do I want today?

Today becomes a fundamental concept in and through cancer treatments. Today is all we have. Today is enough.

The dreams of today have much more to do with the calling dream˜than the visions we cast into an uncertain future. A dream that calls asks you to be more truly yourself, honor your values, strengths, and purposes, all of which you are able to do today.

The dreams we cast into an empty future can become a mask of our true dreams. Our casting dreams become a quest to get to a specific moment we began hoping for years before. This pursuit defines our failures and successes. We set our lives on autopilot, assuming that as long as our trajectory is locked in, we live as we should. Yet, when we pursue a casting dream, we cannot truly experience the fullness of who we are because we are trapped inside a lacking because we have not yet reached that desired moment. The long pursuit causes our days to become routine, and we grind through life tired and half-inspired.

Cancer reveals this facade of a dream. When cancer requires us to stop engaging in the busyness of life, we begin to hear our calling dream, consistent and strong as ever. Listening to this sound is how we learn to begin again.

Following a Dream

After cancer and its treatments, we experience the Void, a season when all the roads of life seem to have disappeared. In these moments, we can begin to feel hopeless, and a new type of uncertainty sets in, worse than the uncertainty of cancer treatments. In the Void, uncertainty is something we would quickly resolve if only we knew how we wanted to proceed. We are filled with questions about ourselves, our identities, and our futures. It is at this moment that we need others more than ever. Whether you are walking out a new dream or one you have chased for many years, it is crucial to have someone who understands the kind of person you want to be, waiting for you at every fork in the road of life.

# Take Action

The cancer experience can leave you with more questions than answers. However, if you answer the questions that swirl in your mind, you may find a way forward. Take your time and honestly answer some of the following:

What has cancer's impact been on my life? What does it mean to my family and friends? Do I want to "go back" to who I was? How do I go forward? Who is currently in my life who understands the kind of person I want to be? How can I lean on this person to help me find my way forward?

What do I truly want from my cancer experience? How do I want this trauma to shape me? What do I want to do with the fear and anxiety that emerged through cancer? It has been said that a person can experience post-traumatic growth. Is this true? If so, what needs to happen in my life?

REFLECTIONS
Grieving the Unknown

I didn't have time to properly experience the Void after stage three treatments because my next traumatic experience with cancer came so quickly. After my treatments for stage three cancer, I had a few wrap-up surgeries, and immediately afterward, I was diagnosed with stage four metastatic cancer. Since I did not have time to grieve this initial change in my life, I was forced to grieve multiple traumas at once.

When I was diagnosed with stage four cancer, I felt like I was moving through a fog. I was disconnected from everyone. Nothing seemed to matter. Every time I said goodbye to someone, it felt like the last goodbye. I did not feel connected, even to myself. The looming future I saw was filled with pain, disappointment, and loss. Every event I could not attend felt like a stabbing knife reminding me of what I had been missing out on these past years and what I will forever miss. There was only cancer and the hurt it created. Even when I could participate, there were constant reminders of how my life was forever changed.

I remember a Christmas when our extended family watched *Dan in Real Life*. It is a story about a man whose wife had died, and he was raising three girls and falling in love again. I left the room and wept. I was inconsolable. It was as if I was getting a glimpse of everyone's future without me. Everything I saw during this season reminded me that I was going to die and everyone else would go on living.

It was the most challenging season of my life. I couldn't continue being the person I was before my diagnosis, and I didn't know if I wanted to be the person I currently was with my diagnosis.

I went to the grocery store and saw a woman I knew well. She looked up and saw me and quickly turned away. It was painfully obvious no one knew what to say when they saw me. This was an additional layer of mourning I had to process. I asked a friend to make me some t-shirts. They said things like, "Nothing is impossible. Even the word itself says I'm possible," a quote by Audrey Hepburn. Or another shirt that said, "Storms make trees take deeper roots," a quote by Dolly Parton. I wanted people to see me and think about something other than cancer. I thought maybe if my shirt sounded hopeful, people wouldn't despair on my behalf. Nonetheless, the season was terrible and hopeless.

Then one day, in the depths of my hurt, I knew I had to let go of my constant state of grieving. In that moment, I chose to hope, despite all the evidence against me. I decided to hope and started declaring hope to anyone who would listen. At that moment, my scans had not gotten any better. There were no new medications to encourage me. The only way out of my despair was to choose a different perspective. Soon afterward, I was at a cancer conference, declaring my hope. I spoke out my hope statement to a man with a booth. The shocking juxtaposition of a young mom with terminal cancer and the hope she declared gripped this man. He listened to me and found my words revolutionary. My words were actively revolutionizing my life too. It was the first moment I found that speaking hope in hopeless situations was liberating, not just to me, but to anyone who would listen. This became my turning point.

One revelatory seed of a thought could take me toward a different future. It was fragile and small, but I felt the possibility. And I didn't want to turn back.

> You are no longer the person you were before cancer, but you have not yet learned who you will be now that life has been impacted by cancer.

CHAPTER 6

Growth

If we imagine something growing and choose one moment in time to define that growing season, it might look like the instant a seed sprouts and pushes up to feel the sun for the first time. It is a vulnerable yet beautiful moment filled with hopeful expectations. Growth has a good reputation. We know that growth should happen throughout life, yet if we stop to think about the experience of growth, these moments are frail and full of uncertainty. Before the plant burst forth, it was a small seed, safely protected by a hard outer shell. A seed could hide away, if necessary, to remain just as it is. It exists in a solid but dormant state. However, when the seed breaks open, the security of the former state is gone, and, in one instant, the fragility of new life emerges.

We can see similar frailties in growing children. As long as babies are carried by their mothers, they remain safe. It is by growing and learning to walk and run that children experience bruised and bloody knees.

Growth is not as easy as it seems. Though it is natural to want to move out of the Void, a season full of life's most uncomfortable moments, we cannot move forward until we have the capacity to endure the bruises that come with growth. The Void is a time to accept the hurts of the past. Until we have truly grieved and released the pain of our prior expectations for life, we are not ready for the disappointments that are experienced in a growing season. Just as a seed will not sprout in the winter, we must wait until the proper time before moving forward into the next stages of healing.

Growth is a fragile, tender season. It is only one step out of the Void. The painful experiences of cancer are in the past, but uncertainty still hangs in the air. Like a late frost in the early spring, there are risks of growing too quickly. A precarious balance must be kept in the early stages of Growth lest heartache and disappointment return. In Growth we feel raw, even in the slightest shifts in the wind, but when the moment passes, our strength rises.

If you are entering the Growth season, it is time for you to begin to design your new identity with the strengths and weaknesses you find in yourself today.

Witnessing Growth

A seed can either remain dormant and secure or come alive and thus become fragile. As humans, we get to make this choice—to stay safe or to become. There seems to be a longing in all of us to experience new things, to grow and change. We are never truly satisfied as dormant creatures. We can witness a child who is learning to walk, and we know that child will fall down quickly after the first step.

Similarly, emotional growth is difficult. The shell that provided emotional protection comes off, walls come down, and you must emerge. You must communicate your transformation. You must find what you need to grow in this emerging state. Those around you, who may be used to you, the dormant seed; their comfort with you in this state may not allow them to encourage you to change. Many people may not know what to think as you first exhibit new colors that demonstrate who you are becoming. However, the shape of your new identity can finally be seen.

There are many different types of growth in nature beyond seedlings. I have seen a young sapling grow out of the stump of an old tree. I have seen an uprooted, fallen tree covered in young bright green branches reaching upward, creating dozens of new trees out of the fallen one. I have seen redwoods with burls on their side that cover the scars of long-ago fires. These burls can be covered with hundreds of baby redwoods growing together, connected not only to the mother tree but also to the root system of every tree in the grove. I have seen a mountainside that has been burned. Black spikes remain from the trees that existed before the fires, and just below their midpoint are huge bushes growing. Each tree is restoring its life above ground. The tree's life was not destroyed; it was safe because what could not be seen remained, even through a devastating natural disaster. It remained safe because its strength always existed under the surface, supporting the trees we knew and loved. We often mourn the loss of vegetation after a fire, but what was lost was just the portion of the forest that we are familiar with. There is so much more hidden deep below.

You may have been to a naturalist museum and seen an exhibit demonstrating a tree's root system. If you have, it is an unforgettable experience. Trees are just as big underground as they are above. Their root systems stretch below the surface, providing strength, stability, and life for the tree we see. A fire cannot permeate into the soil. It cannot destroy the tree's true source of strength. For this reason, after every mountain catches fire, life begins again. Life begins in the same spot where it was taken away. These deeply rooted trees grow again and again. I think it is important to recognize the fires in life can only burn and destroy what is above the surface. It can only damage what is on the outside. No matter what the disaster is, our roots remain safe.

Uncovering Our Roots

The trees of the forest are in a constant state of change. Winter, spring, and fall all cause the trees to undergo change. Leaves fall to the ground leaving nothing but sticks and twigs. Spring brings tiny buds that eventually burst forth into leaves and flowers. In autumn, if the trees have been well-fed during the summer, their leaves will take on beautiful colors. When seen in a community with other trees, the beauty of a forest in color is unrivaled. On the other hand, if the tree has not received rain through the summer, the leaves dry on the branch.

Just like what we witness in nature, our outward identities are in a constant state of change. Others notice this change, even if we pretend it is not happening. Growing up and growing old do not happen overnight, though often it feels that way. We are very good at pretending that our outward selves are safe, secure, and unshifting when the opposite is quite evident.

Conversely, our rooted selves only become stronger over time. When given the proper conditions, our inward selves forever establish the ability to remain resilient and safe. Our rooted selves are stretching outward, going deeper, searching for ways to better support and grow what can be seen outwardly.

Growth feels impossibly difficult at first. Impossibly difficult. We do not know what we are becoming, yet we feel the need to grow.

Most of us have not needed to rely on our rooted self, or true identity. We have allowed our identity to become only what is above ground, what others can see. An identity based on the outward will always lead to disappointment. The years of life change the outward identity of every one of us. Through age, trauma, or disease, we are guaranteed to lose that outward person of our youth eventually. However, cancer wipes away the outward identity suddenly. When disasters in life damage our outward identity, we have an opportunity to re-discover the part of us that remains. Our roots, our foundation, our inward identity cannot be destroyed by outward forces.

When my children were young and I was going through surgeries and chemo, I would regularly have conversations with them about the changes happening in my body.

I would ask, "If I lose my hair, will I still be your mother?"

"Yes, Mom," they'd say.

"If the doctor cuts off my breast, will I still love you?"

"Of course, Mom."

"Is there any way cancer or the doctor can change my body and it will change who I am on the inside?"

Quietly considering the question, "I guess not."

"That is right, there is no surgeon's knife, or radiation beam, or needle that can make me, Lauren, your mom, into a different person. I will always be your mother. I will always love you. We don't have to be afraid."

Even children understand that who we are has nothing to do with how we look. There is something more to the person that we see. There are roots deep beneath the surface directing our character, integrity, and love. Though we know this, it is easy to forget when the part of us that is seen experiences unexpected physical trauma. It is easy to think we have lost ourselves. It is easy to hide because our outward identity cannot be found. It is easy to focus on what can be seen and forget that unshakable roots are inside, waiting to burst with life.

Self-Discovery

The Growth season is a period of self-discovery. It is the season when you remember where your strength comes from, and you discover new strengths you picked up in and through cancer. It is a time for testing your boundaries and stretching beyond what you feel is possible. This season of emerging is not about knowing all the answers. You will remain uncertain during this season. Uncertain but hopeful.

Uncertainty in the Void was tied to fear. Uncertainty now, in Growth, is pulled by hope. Like a leaf stretching toward the sun, something draws us outward, beyond our hiding places. The season of Growth is typically fueled by a single thought that cannot be shaken. It is driven by something deep within that is rooted in our core. Perhaps it has always been present, but its shape and form were hidden, or perhaps it is something new.

This single thought is present when we wake up and in the peaceful moments of the day. It is powerful and can drive away the fear that continues to creep back into our minds. Allow this thought room to grow. Remember, our roots give us stability and feed our outward growth. To grow outward, we must invest in our inward growth.

Growth is raw and bright, and full of purpose. It is a season with more questions than answers. These questions are not the same questions that filled your mind during the early days of cancer. These questions feed your soul and give you strength. They can be lined up like little branches stretching you toward the light.

When these branches reach toward the warmth of hope, you experience growth. Without knowing it, these sprouts, feeling their way outward, cause something new to emerge in who you are. You become the beautiful, delicate being that emerged from a tiny, closed-off seed.

Hope That Fuels Growth

This emergent being is the inward you, demonstrating the parts of you that could not be broken. These parts have always been just below the surface. Now that the outward identity is gone, the inward identity continues doing what it has always done, supporting you. Emerging from trauma and disappointment of the darkness, now the inward identity begins pushing toward the light of hope.

I don't believe a seed knows what potential it holds. If seeds were certain of their next form, they would burst with excitement of what will be. Similarly, though you may not recognize the stirring in your heart, do not disqualify its value. Everything in life is built one step at a time, so you must continue to move forward. Listen well to yourself.

When you tune into your inner strength, at first it might be hard to distinguish between the raw sensation of newness and the former sensation of pain. Emotions are not often easily categorized. Listen to yourself and see if the emotion grows in pain or grows in purpose. Similarly, the presence of uncertainty might shift, from feeling uncertain about any future, to feeling uncertain about the future you are choosing. Listen closely to yourself with the type of joyful expectation that bubbles up whenever you have the privilege to view the birth of something new.

Envision the seedling that you are, then give this emerging identity the honored space to grow.

Growing Hope

Hope is a powerful force that should never remain stagnant. As we grow, our hope must grow. When we are uncertain about cancer and our future, our hope needs only to be big enough to help us take one step closer to certainty. Then when we fully embrace who we want to be, our hope must be borderline irrational—we must fully expect that every good thing will surround and carry us forward. It is only with a perspective filled with hope that we can step into the unknown potential of our lives. Though we feel this potential, the road has not been walked before, and every step feels uncertain. Hope reminds us of what it is we are living for and makes uncertainty an acceptable part of the process.

Growth does not happen quickly or in great measures. Leaps that take us from where we are to somewhere completely new are not probable. Small steps, on the other hand, toe-to-heal steps, determine the trajectory of our lives. These forward movements occur daily, in every decision and in every interaction with others.

The opposite of hope is fear. Fear is known to cause a fight, flight, or freeze response. Fear stops us in our tracks and can cause us to run backward, away from who we want to be. Hope, on the other hand, is growth. It expands us beyond our current boundaries, beyond what we can see today. Once we learn to identify our roots, the hidden identity that is safe inside us, we can grow resilient. This inner identity is unshakable. When fear emerges, which it will, returning to that inward identity eases our fears. The rooted identity remained throughout the trauma of cancer, and it is strong enough to withstand the uncertainty of growth.

Our emotional growth is difficult to track because it doesn't reveal itself in a pair of old shoes growing snug. Change is occurring within us. Just as a doctor will measure a child's height to measure growth, we need a tool to assess the development of our hope. The level of our hope directs our thoughts and indicates our emotional resilience. Just as a doctor will listen to our heartbeat to indicate our physical vitality, hope is a rhythmic pulse indicating our emotional strength.

So how do we measure hope? When considering hope, we must assess, "Is my hope passive or active?" Passive hope is a wish list. It takes the shape of a childhood story that leaves us waiting for a solution to emerge just as a fairy might become visible after making a wish on a star. This hope lives outside of our control or influence. It is something we might watch for but would not pursue. Active hope feels vibrant, as if that which we hope is already true, we must only continue down our path to find it. Active hope is like a hike in the forest knowing there is a waterfall to be found at the end of the trail. We must walk the path; the waterfall will not come to us. However, we know, with confidence, that if we continue down the path, we will see the waterfall that has been envisioned. Passive hope is stagnant, a waiting process with no relationship to our actions. Active hope is an assurance that keeps us moving with joyful expectation.

Is your hope passive or active?

Are you on the lookout for that which you hope?

Do you feel as if your hope could be realized around the next bend of the trail?

What are you doing to actualize this hope?

Urgency of the Day

When looking at life, it seems as if there is a distant tomorrow that will be important. But today, it is what we have, it is not disposable. Today is significant and should not be overlooked.

Cancer and other traumas break the concept that a distant tomorrow holds the greatest value of life. Today is important. Even the mundane routines of today are meaningful. Those mundane routines make up the majority of life. Car rides to and from school with your children, time at work with co-workers, dinners around the table, and bedtime routines become the spaces where most of life is lived. They are beautiful opportunities to love well, live purposefully, and find contentment.

When Adventure Therapy Foundation gifts a retreat to families impacted by cancer, we intentionally send those families somewhere within three hours of where they live. I tell them, "Anyone can be happy in Fiji, but it is more important that we learn to be happy right where we are."

Where are you today? The place you are right now has a sunrise and a sunset, yet how often do you step outside and observe it? What other beauty are you missing out on because you may bury your thoughts inside of our expectations for the routines of tomorrow?

Living with metastatic breast cancer creates an urgency in me. The urgency does not come from a fear of dying. It comes from the value I place upon today. Today is beautiful. Today is significant. And I have just as much potential to bring change today as tomorrow or any day following. The only requirement is to reach out and understand what is here. Living urgently is not based on fear, it is based on seeing the value of where I am.

If I were on vacation in Hawaii, I would wake up early every day. Excited to go out and explore the spaces around me. The knowledge that my time there was short would make my senses come alive and give me the motivation to go and do all that I can do. Living urgently feels like this. Waking up every day, excited about what I might discover. A day in Hawaii might bring rain or too much sun, but we do not worry about that. We simply embrace the good. Yet in our mundane and everyday lives, we spend our energy looking at what might go wrong rather than right.

Living urgently allows you to value today. Today is a good day to be with your family. Today is a good day to reach out to a friend. Today is a good day to make things right with those who have hurt you. This type of living helps eliminate the regrets of tomorrow.

A life well-lived might be realized at sixty-five, a time when one has enough space to look back and reflect on the full landscape of a life. It might have been acknowledged at sixty-five, but it didn't begin there. A well-lived life is built one moment at a time, one decision at a time, and one day at a time.

How are your decisions shaping your life? Like seeds scattered along our path, we may not see the impact of the decisions we make right away. Our daily decisions feel small and overlooked, yet, every moment is a seed, small but holding the potential for so much more. Living an urgent life is like looking at a tiny seed and seeing the flower it will become or looking at a moment and seeing its ripples. To live urgently means not holding anything back, to always be in motion—forward in love, healing, and purpose. By doing what can be done today, the regrets in life grow small.

This type of urgency defines my intentions, not my actions. To live at a frantic pace with a busy schedule is not the type of urgency that we're talking about here. In fact, living an urgently intentional life often requires us to slow down what we do. Living an urgently intentional life after a cancer diagnosis means we take time to absorb every moment. It means we do not waste the beauty that is available to us. From an outside perspective, living urgently might look like slowing down because a slower pace allows us to observe the good available in life. A busy life requires that we pass by the daily small beauties as we head to the next big thing. An urgently intentional life has the capacity to find gratitude for every moment of life.

When life is shaped by perpetually running a little late, a culture of lacking becomes part of our perspective. This sense of lacking time bleeds into our sense of not fulfilling roles and responsibilities. If we don't have enough time to fit it all in, then something must get pushed to the side for us to be successful. Typically, what gets passed over are family dinners around the table, and peaceful evenings filled with laughter and conversation. On our way to do all the things, we find the most important things are feeling further and further away. This only perpetuates the lacking sensation. While we work, day and night, running the road, we find ourselves caught in an ever-growing cycle of lacking. While we find ways to check off every task on our list, the desires of our hearts grow dimmer. Connection and relationship take a backseat to tasks and responsibilities.

On my podcast I ask those impacted by cancer, "What is the gift of cancer? What did you learn from the cancer experience that was a gift in your life?" The answer over and over is, "I have learned to slow down. I have learned to appreciate the people in my life. I have learned to be thankful for today." Today is here, and it is filled with abundant opportunities. Value what you have. We must not waste our energy, emotion, and time, mourning for what might not be.

Pruning Pain

Life is complicated. Chances are cancer is not the first trauma you have faced. So what do you do if what grows in this new season triggers more pain, pain from previous traumas in life?

In nature, we know that the plants that grow in a particular micro-ecosystem will support the other plants growing in that same space. So the tall trees provide shade for the underbrush, and the small plants enrich the soil allowing the trees to grow taller. While we can acknowledge and understand this interdependence found in nature, we often ignore the *micro-emosystems* found in our own lives and in our emotions.

exploring the seasons of emotional healing

The anger, disappointment, disgust, sadness, and other emotions experienced in cancer are connected in our inner identity to prior experiences of anger, disappointment, disgust, and sadness. Therefore, if we have experienced moments in life of extreme disappointment, and we left those moments unresolved, then the new circumstance of cancer will spark disappointment that is not only attached to this circumstance but has also connected us to all the previous disappointments where this emotion showed up. The roots of disappointment that weave throughout our lives will quickly create a compounded pain in the present circumstance. We will not truly be able to grow in a healthy way until all experiences of disappointment have been properly grieved and released.

Brambles are a nuisance in a forest, their thorns cut curious wanderers and send them packing home. These brambles will grow and grow inside a forest even if the branches are removed. If you trim a path through the brambles, the roots will quickly grow new sprouts, and in a matter of weeks, it will seem as if you never cleared a path at all. Unless the roots of the brambles are dug up, this forest will never be enjoyable for fear of the thorns. Similarly, if throughout our lives, we have only dealt with disappointment as it is seen in our outward identity, there is a good chance the roots of those painful memories continue to grow and expand in our inner identity.

Dealing with the branches of disappointment as they are connected to your cancer story will not truly free you from the presence of their pain. You must dig deeper. The roots of your emotions are interconnected to other disappointing and traumatic circumstances if the roots of those past events were never properly acknowledged.

As we grieve and release the pain of our past experiences, we find the tools to repeat this process until the thorny brambles in our emo-system are cleared out. Only then are we free to face future hardships and disappointments without fear of relapsing into old patterns of pain.

Take Action

Use this season to begin to look ahead. Who do you want to be? What do you want to become?

Looking at the life you have lived, where do you see brambles of pain growing in your emo-system? The system of your emotions and strengths are connected just as the branches of brambles are connected through a root system. What is emotionally enriching to you? How are these emotionally enriching areas growing in your life? Are you making these a priority? As you consider your life, like an eco-system, consider all that is needed to ensure a thriving forest exists. Consider your great strengths, that grow like trees for all to see. Consider the small, fragile ideas of your life that are growing in the shade of your established strengths. Think of how these small ideas are supporting and enriching your established strengths. Think of the painful brambles. Remember, no matter how strong or lush your forest appears, you will never be able to enjoy a pain-free experience exploring this life until these brambles are uprooted.

exploring the seasons of emotional healing

> Draw a picture of a forest. Label each tree, underbrush, weed, and bug with your own strengths, pain-points, curiosities, and fragile yet enriching ideas. Allow this picture of an eco-system to be a reminder of your emo-system. You are connected to your experience, past and present. You are growing, and each new seed, new sprout, or new leaf needs space and resources to grow. What can you do in your own emo-system to facilitate that growth?

The Spectrum of Hope assessment tool is designed to demonstrate our personal hope levels. The Spectrum of Hope measures our emotional capacity for risk, resilience, and emotional growth. Where are you on the Spectrum of Hope?

Spectrum of Hope

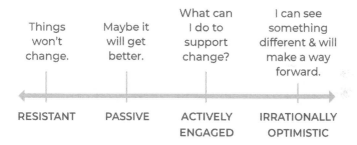

REFLECTIONS

Learning to Carry Uncertainty

after my metastatic diagnosis, I chose to embrace a vision of my future that didn't involve immediate death. Once I resolved that I had a future to live in, I needed to know where to direct my life. I was walking a brand-new path. None of my friends or family could understand my course or walk it with me. I had no experience in this space and no one to offer me wisdom. Once I set aside the idea of dying, nothing else felt very scary. So I started taking risks I would never have taken before.

A stranger in an airport offered to do the legal work to establish a nonprofit for me. In the past, taking favors from strangers was akin to taking candy from strangers—you probably should not do it. In this situation, I uncharacteristically said, "Yes, please do!" Then other strangers offered me money for my nonprofit. Every day I woke up and took one more step on my new path. Every day I had no idea where I was going or how I would get there. I helped one person at a time, listened to one broken heart at a time, and before long, I was impacting lives. My

> "Living an urgent life is like looking at a tiny seed and seeing the flower it will become or looking at a moment and seeing its ripples. By doing what can be done today, the regrets in life grow small."

heart was still raw, but others found my rawness to affirm that their pain was understood. My decisions were still unsure, but my passion filled in the gaps where knowledge failed. I kept moving one step further on a path I was creating. Growth is filled with uncertainty, but cancer has taught me how to carry uncertainty.

For years I woke up and took the next step, any step I could take. By following my heart day after day, I found my heart had a path it was walking, even if my mind didn't fully understand it. My Growth season had nothing to do with logic; I had to walk through life from the heart. My pre-cancer life had been about responsibility, but in this early season of Growth, I needed freedom to take risks of my own design.

> "Living an urgently intentional life after a cancer diagnosis means we take time to absorb every moment."

CHAPTER 7

Restoration

If the Growth season is represented by the seedling of your new identity emerging from the dark soil, then the season of Restoration is where you move from a delicate sprout into a firmly established tree. Restoration is the season when you find your strength. No longer are you filled with questions about who you will be. The lessons of each of the previous seasons of healing gave you clarity that you did not possess at the beginning of this process. Now you have done the difficult work of pushing through Growth, and you have emerged in your new identity. Since you have broken through every obstacle, and through a fragile beginning declared your new identity, you can now establish the person you are becoming.

Restoration is a time to practice living a new way. Through practice you begin to build strength. This rhythm of living into your new identity begins to dim the rhythms of life before cancer. As you embrace your new mindset, intentionality, and values, you will find your inner identity and outward identity becoming one and the same. This alignment will help you grow in awareness that you are on a path that is uniquely yours. Sure of the person you have become, you can move toward the purposes of your heart. This repeated intentionality will restore you and even provide you with opportunities that were not available before cancer.

This season returns you to those pre-diagnosis moments of assurance. While your new strength and your pre-cancer strength feel similar, they will have many differences. Your pre-trauma strength was grounded in innocence. At that time, you felt certain about what you would accomplish today, next week, next year, and for the rest of your life. Knowing what you wanted for your future provided you with strength. Your confidence in what the future would bring gave you direction. The trauma of cancer erased all of those plans, but during your pre-cancer life, these untested plans were your foundation.

Today, you have a new foundation, not a foundation of innocence but one that is deeply rooted. You have walked through fire. You have re-established yourself. You have grown. Today you are rooted, firm, and secure for the first time since diagnosis. Today's strength comes from a deep knowing, from experiencing trials, and from choosing to heal. There is a certainty available to you for the first time in many seasons. This certainty comes from the choices you have made, the choices you will make, day after day, to keep going—the choice to pursue healing rather than hide in pain. Often, the most formative decisions of your life are tiny choices made in repetition. You have chosen hope over fear, a small yet mighty choice. These choices have rooted you and given you the ability to grow. You have established thought patterns that enrich your emo-system. These thoughts now fertilize your life with hope and fill you with purpose. You have removed many of the pain points from your heart. By addressing these disappointments and painful circumstances, you are able to walk through life with less pain. You have aligned your inner identity with your outward identity. Now you can walk whole and complete. You are stronger than ever because of the season of healing that followed cancer.

Purpose and intention feed your new identity, and the fruit of these thoughts will continue to make seeds that establish an intentional life and a hopeful future. You have learned to stop the cycle of craving certainty. You have learned to turn away from fear when your circumstances unravel. You have learned to accept that you cannot control where cancer may or may not be, but you can control how you spend every moment. You have tested these theories and are confident that when life disappoints you, you will not live in regret. You choose to live well. You choose not to hide beneath the surface. You choose not to let fear control your identity. Restoration is a season of establishing strength of mind and, hopefully, peace of mind. It is a pivotal season where you find the capacity to begin to stretch outward, growing fruit and shade that will, in the future, provide refuge for others.

This is restoration, and restoration is a treasure.

Restoration of Others

As you have been moving through the seasons of healing, those who love you have been doing the same. Your loved ones have been watching and waiting for a sign that everything will be okay, a sign only you can provide them. The sign that everything will be okay might look like you laughing without hesitation, or they might feel your strength when they notice you listening and remaining emotionally available. These signs give your family permission to begin to breathe a sigh of relief.

Restoration is a season where others can feel safe to verbalize their curiosity about your experience of cancer. In the previous season, the work you were doing was underground, internal, and hidden.

You were finding words, finding direction, finding purpose in the pain. Now, in Restoration, you are emerging in a way that those who love you can begin to understand. It is now that they can begin to see the true impact of the emotional side effects of cancer.

By doing the difficult work of healing, you have demonstrated what true strength looks like, and those you love have had a front seat to witness your strength. This has not been lost to those around you. Before now they may not have verbalized their observations because they did not know if the process of pain was complete. However, in the Restoration season, those who love you will begin to feel safe too. You will be shocked as those who you felt were on the fringes of your life begin to share their admiration for how you have inspired them. There will be moments and conversations you have forgotten that have taken root in the hearts of others. They will now bring these thoughts to you and offer them back to you as a gift of their admiration. As your strength grows and your restoration process becomes more evident, your restoration will feed the seeds that have been planted in the hearts of others. As you experience restoration, you will discover hope growing in more hearts than you ever knew.

Strength is not a word that defines actions done with ease. Strength is demonstrated with great effort, strain, sweat, and tears. At this moment, you may not consider yourself strong. You may not feel the strength others have witnessed. Those around you saw you struggle. They saw you fail, yet you walked back into the process again and again. They saw you struggle with hope and fear, and they see you now. It is through the pursuit of healing that you demonstrate strength. Others are inspired by the pursuit. It is not the perfect execution of unlimited strength that causes others to be inspired, instead they are inspired by how you use the limited strength you have when facing impossible situations. As others face what they feel to be impossible situations, they remember your pursuit. When they are required to live in uncertainty, they can access a seed of hope that took root in their identity through observing you.

When someone comments on our strength in and through cancer, it is easy to brush such a statement aside. Rarely do we feel strong. However, strength is not limited to the physical; we have little control over whether our bodies will fight cancer. Strength is walking through the darkest of situations and not resigning. Perhaps you stopped treatment or cried in bed for a whole day. This does not negate your strength. This is the struggle; this is the work. Strength is continuing to love when every bit of life is against you. Strength is hoping against hope that things can get better. Strength is continuing forward when nothing but hardship awaits you. Strength is choosing to smile, getting dressed, sitting at the table, and showing up. You carry a beautiful strength, even when you feel weak. This is what your family sees when they look at your face. Your friends refer to this when they tell you how strong you are. This is your legacy, how you have taught others to face hardships with strength and purpose.

Restòring Expectations

Your family and friends have become very good at watching you closely. My daughters still watch me closely even though it has been years since my initial treatment. If I moan or groan in a new way, they are quick to define and diagnose what is causing my complaints, which is often just me being lazy. Your family is watching you closely, and in the season of Restoration, their observations can cause conflict.

Your family expects you to be the person they knew pre-cancer. They do not know the trauma of cancer has changed you. Those who love you might only be able to observe this shift in your identity for the first time in the Restoration season. While you have been processing uncertainty, so has your family. To those around you, this emerging post-cancer version of you will feel like a continuation of their uncertainty. You must introduce your family to your intentional self. While another change in their lives will feel unsettling at first, as soon as they see this new version of you is stronger, happier, and more capable of living well, they will embrace what is best for you.

Your family will not understand your new perspective right away. This transition in you has taken significant time and effort. It is important for you to take time to clearly communicate with those you love. You must be honest with your family. Leaving your internal shift unspoken will result in an ongoing conflict. As you find your post-cancer trajectory, talk about it with those you love. They too might need permission to adjust their life's path. Everything you are able to put into words will teach your loved ones how they might overcome trauma in a healthy, restorative way. Your children may not have cancer one day, but they will face hardships. Teaching them the tools that have helped you will make them resilient throughout their life.

When we get married, we often say "for better or for *worse.*" While this line applies to marriage, family is also for better or worse. It is easy to share the better parts of our lives with those we love, but sometimes we question how much of the "worse" needs to be known. Allowing your family to learn about the emotional side effects of cancer will empower them. They have witnessed every day of your treatment and restoration. They too have emotional side effects of cancer and need the tools to process cancer's impact on their lives. Sharing your stories will help acknowledge the deep hurts they carry from life. You did not stop at worse. You pursued wellness until you were able to heal from the trauma of cancer. They will be strengthened by your healing, and their strength is your legacy.

Even if we know it is the right thing to do, it is hard to talk about our cancer experience with those we love. Much like the experience of cancer, the healing from cancer can feel like an emotional rollercoaster. We might report to our family that we feel restored, and then the following day we feel as if the trauma is beginning all over. Cancer is painful, and its ripples continue throughout life. It hurts every time a friend is diagnosed. We have to relive our own traumas at each scan. Our cancerversary can be a celebration or a time of grief. The presence and pain points of cancer are hard to predict. Just because we have reached Restoration does not mean every hurt has been erased. However, remember our definition of strength. It is only by doing difficult things that we demonstrate true strength. By doing the difficult work of healing, we can live a testimony of hope for others walking through their own traumas. We can provide shade during the scorching heat of disappointment. We can stand on the strength of our experiences and help others when they have no strength. Achieving restoration is very personal, but it is a gift that extends far beyond ourselves. A purposeful future is the greatest gift of hope we can offer.

Take Action

Celebrate this season!

We had ideas of who we wanted to become when we were young. We pursued this at some level, but responsibilities and choices zig-zagged us along our path, and most of us found our attention, time, and talents splintered. Yet we celebrated every milestone.

We celebrated graduation, marriage, new babies, new jobs, new houses. In our pre-cancer life we knew we were stepping into new seasons of life because they were typical and familiar.

Then, cancer charred every part of life. It cleared the thicket of tasks and responsibilities that made up our schedules and expectations.

However, once the fires passed, we were able to find new opportunities. Instead of random layers of brush filling our lives, we have a clean slate. We have permission to start again. Now, we are able to curate the gardens of our lives with greater wisdom. We have the opportunity to reengage in what we find beautiful and fulfilling.

Yes, it may take some time to uncover the parts of us that could not be shaken. However, in the ashes we find the good in the experience of cancer. It is where the gifts of life are hidden. It is here we learn that we have arrived in a purposeful future. Restoration is a time to rebuild, to look beyond our circumstances, and to move confidently toward an uncertain future. This season of Restoration becomes a bud of hope for others. Living a life that embraces post-traumatic growth is as beautiful to observe as a new spring flower. By choosing to heal, we demonstrate how beauty can emerge from ashes. Such a transformation inspires those we love to find what they need to make their dreams grow too.

So take some time and celebrate!

REFLECTIONS

Embracing Passionate Living

Once I established my path, I began to dream beyond the next twenty-four hours. I found a new trajectory for my life, so I began to test just how far that trajectory might reach. In my season of Restoration, I took the path my heart established and started to build structures and strategies so my path might go far beyond myself or my lifetime. My resources were few, but I used this season to lay the groundwork for something bigger than myself.

My first step was to create a nonprofit. I founded Adventure Therapy Foundation and immediately began supporting families and their struggles around emotional side effects of cancer. Then I knew I needed to get my philosophy of cancer out of my brain and into the world. If I did this, I knew Adventure Therapy would always have the tools it needed to continue, with or without me. I started doing this with a podcast, *Adventures with Scars,* and began writing this book. The book took me more than a year to write, and during this process, I began traveling and speaking on my philosophy. Instead of feeling fulfilled by these accomplishments, my vision only got bigger. I dreamt of ways every person impacted by cancer could have access to tools that minimize the fear, isolation, and broken identity of cancer. I began building an app, planned curriculum that could educate the whole family, established digital educational materials on Adventure Therapy's website, and on and on my thoughts continued. Today I feel more sure of this path than ever.

I expect this will be the task I work on for the rest of my life. I have found my life's work and will now pursue new ways to reach as many people impacted by cancer as possible. As I work to bring others into a season of Restoration, I use my pain and story to move forward. This is where my restoration takes root. I no longer need to protect myself. Every day is filled with intentional living,

> **This repeated intentionality will restore you and even provide you with opportunities that were not available before cancer.**

and the threat of death cannot squelch the joy of living well. I live a life in the service of others that grows out of my own weaknesses, my own Fire season.

This purpose gets me up early in the morning, full of possibilities that run through my mind all day long. It makes me bold and requires that I take risks, not for myself but in the service of others. Just as strength is defined by the struggle, my impact, in many ways, will be defined not by my level of success, but instead the pursuit of purpose. Those who know me and observe my life will not be shaken if I do not successfully reach every human impacted by cancer. They will, however, be changed by a life fully committed to passionate living.

CHAPTER 8

Giving

While walking the Camino de Santiago, I carried everything I needed on my back. Every day, I woke up and asked the question: What exactly do I need? The answer to that question was constantly changing. On some days, I needed to carry three liters of water, while on others, I only needed to take thirty-two ounces. The difference between these two amounts is nearly five pounds. Five pounds is a lot of unnecessary weight to carry for eight hours and sixteen miles!

When we do the work of letting go of unnecessary burdens, we have an increase in capacity. One strategic decision I made on the 200-mile walk of the Camino was to take only one pair of shoes. I did not want to carry an extra pair of shoes in my bag during my whole journey. On my most difficult day of hiking, I found a pair of shoes on the trail. I knew everyone on this trail was only carrying what they needed, and if someone dropped this pair, it would be very important they get the shoes back. I picked up the shoes without hesitation, tied them to my pack, and continued. I carried those shoes over multiple mountain ranges until I came to a small town at dusk. Despite my absolute exhaustion, I immediately went to work locating the shoes' owner. I didn't know who they might belong to, so I had to continue to walk, asking everyone I saw. When I found the man who lost them, I found a friend for life. Though we spoke different languages, he managed to explain that these were his only shoes (he was riding a bike and only had cycling shoes). He told me if I hadn't carried these shoes off the mountain, he would have had to walk around in yellow flip-flops all over the gothic city of Santiago.

At this moment, I realized I had chosen not to carry the weight of a second pair of shoes for myself, yet I was willing to carry the shoes for another. Carrying these shoes for one day seemed like a small burden, while carrying my shoes for the full 200-mile trek was not a weight I was willing to bear. Yet, I carried this burden on my most difficult day without hesitation because it was in the service of another. Then after the most difficult hike of my life, I refused to rest until I found the shoes' owner. Caring for the need of another, someone I didn't even know, taught me I am stronger than I think.

Shaping Ourselves for the Good of Others

When we do the work of letting go of our disappointments and broken expectations, we have the capacity to carry the burdens of others. By holding space within ourselves, by leaving that space empty and below capacity, we have the ability to support others. If we protect a space within ourselves, we have the capacity to relieve the burdens of others and ensure they have the strength to continue.

The beautiful thing about relieving the burdens of others is that five pounds of hurt to someone else is only a temporary burden to me. Knowing it is mine to carry for only a short time, I can bear their burdens much more easily. I can receive what they cannot carry, which is the greatest gift we can offer another person.

Giving by Receiving

By releasing five pounds of worry or fear in your own life, you can make space for five pounds of something new. For this to happen, you must perpetually reevaluate your needs.

On the Camino, my needs changed every day, and I have found, in my regular living, my needs do the same. I know myself enough to recognize there are seasons I need more support and seasons when I can invest in others. For example, my cancerversary is November 11, and my second diagnosis was on December 21. During the season between November 1 and January 1, I feel frail. I may not melt down at every turn, but I have a very small capacity to carry the burdens of another. The rhythms of that season remind me of the dramatic changes that occurred in my life. Memories and disappointments can distract me throughout the holidays. However, once the New Year comes, all of that is behind me, and I can and will do anything to relieve the burdens of someone else. It isn't logical for me to feel this way, but that has been my emotional experience throughout the years. This shift isn't perceivable to others, so I have to do a good job reminding those I love of this shift in my capacity. This is an example of when my life has little capacity. At other times of the year, I might carry the burdens of a dozen people at once without feeling overwhelmed.

Our shifting capacity can only be utilized when we look honestly at ourselves on a regular basis. Creating an increase in capacity provides us with so much potential! It can be filled with personal risks and responsibilities, or we can choose to leave it temporarily empty until something meaningful emerges. It can also be left empty indefinitely, allowing us the ability to remain available to help others.

Holding space to increase your emotional capacity is not the same as the emptiness experienced in the Void. In the Void, you had no capacity. You were hurting. There was space all around you, but no emotional capacity. In the Giving season, your identity has been restored, and this emotional space is a gift for you to use as you desire.

What Giving Means to Others

Cancer and its treatments are burdens that compound over the treatment process and into early survivorship. As treatments linger, the emotional and physical exhaustion multiplies. During this time, a survivor is asked to bear more than ever, physically, emotionally, and financially. When someone who understands the disappointments and burdens of cancer comes to their side, these two survivors can bear the burdens of cancer together. Carrying even small portions of the grief provides great relief to an overburdened friend. When we commit ourselves to the healing journey of an early survivor, our presence ensures they never experience the isolation, fear, and brokenness we were required to endure. Our presence stops the full impact of the emotional side effects of cancer, relieves their burdens, and reduces the scars they will carry. By standing with someone as they heal, we give them the gift of life; because when we decrease another's emotional burden, they require less time to heal. With less time needed to heal, they are given more time to live. Our gift does not stop there, by minimizing their emotional side effects, we minimize cancer's impact on their loved ones as well. The simple act of showing up for someone can minimize or eliminate the ripples of cancer for generations.

The gift of time should be an impossible gift to offer someone. It is a gift outside of our ability to produce, but sacrificial giving tends to grow exponentially, making the gift of life itself a gift within our grasp.

Giving Hope

Giving looks different for everyone because we are all unique. Giving means using what is uniquely you for the sake of someone else.

I love photography, so I support Adventure Therapy Foundation by saving some of my best images for the annual art walk. One survivor loves crafting and making cards, so she sells those cards and donates the money to support her local charity. Another co-survivor is a great organizer. She can take a chaotic level of donations, put them into an appealing system, and raise money through raffle baskets. There is a business owner who is a co-survivor with tons of connections, and she uses these to bring awareness.

Many survivors share their stories, creating confidence in patients. One cancer patient loves to ride motorcycles. She takes a ride once a year to raise awareness, build relationships, and raise money for her favorite charity. On and on, the uniqueness of who we are becomes the perfect piece of the puzzle for someone else. Small assistance from one person's perspective can be a hope-giving, life-extending restoration to another. Never underestimate a small act of kindness.

What Giving Means to You

Serving others without expecting anything in return creates a sense of belonging, confidence, and strength in both individuals. To give is to take an active role, to join a community in deed and not just in word. Giving is one of the truly satisfying things we can do in life. It reminds us of how we are all responsible for the life others experience. It teaches us just how we are abundantly cared for. It gives us confidence in the amount of emotional and physical strength we own. It is a guarantee that good things are available. Giving is a gift to us as well as others.

In this season, find innovative ways to support your community. Don't feel like you must check a box or take action in a generic way. Giving can be deeply meaningful for you, so embrace the experience. Giving reminds you of how much you have grown. When caring for another, you are reminded of how difficult the experience of cancer truly was. This reminder, especially after healing has occurred, acts as an encouragement. You really did go through something very difficult! You really were filled with questions and uncertainty day and night. You were in their shoes and now look at how far you have come! Even if the present doesn't feel perfect, healing has happened, and you are not the same person you were at the time of diagnosis.

Helping others provides an opportunity to reflect. When we went through cancer treatments, we didn't have answers for the questions that filled our minds. Now when others ask those same questions, we have a lot more answers. We were growing, even when we didn't know it. All of that hard-earned knowledge and wisdom we gained through treatments is just sitting in our hearts and minds waiting for a purpose. Helping others can give our experience purpose. As we lean into the lives of others, we often find meaning in our painful memories of cancer.

Take Action

The season of Giving is only available to us if we increase our emotional capacity. If you consider Taking Every Thought Captive (as discussed in Chapter Three) as an introduction to renewing your mind, then holding space is more like renewing your mind 2.0.

While Taking Every Thought Captive is practiced for the sake of our own mental well-being, holding space is not necessarily self-serving but instead is practiced for the sake of others. Holding space does benefit the individual, for the space we create allows for our own rest, reflection, and renewal. However, over a lifetime of practice, this tool guarantees we have the capacity to welcome others into our lives, even if their life is in a season of Fire.

We are only able to hold space in ourselves if we practice laying down what no longer serves us. We have moved through many seasons of healing. The emotions, thoughts, and burdens we picked up when our lives were in a season of Fire are not relevant to us in a season of Restoration. By laying those burdens down, we find an increased capacity within.

Cancer took your life in an unexpected direction. Therefore, your emotional capacity is probably still impacted by broken expectations from your pre-cancer life.

Grab your journal. Reflect on your pre-cancer ideas around relationships, finances, goals, and productivity. Write down broken expectations that feel unresolved or incomplete.

The acknowledgment of these losses might stir up grief. Disappointment and grief are emotional burdens. Take time to truly reflect on your life, writing as much as possible. Keeping grief and disappointment inside of you only ensures you continue to carry these burdens further into life than necessary.

After releasing your broken expectations and processing your grief, you should feel an increase in yourself. Exactly like taking a loaded backpack off your back, you might feel relief and a sense of being lighter. If you do not, keep digging! Continue to unload your burdens until this sense of relief is present.

Creating space is just the beginning. In truth, every day creates new broken expectations. These pain points may seem small compared to the broken experience of cancer, but those daily disappointments accumulate inside of you. Make a practice of acknowledging life's grief and brokenness. Unload these disappointments as often as possible. There is no benefit for you to continue to carry them through life. Holding space is an ongoing commitment to protect the emotional space we created.

Protect and defend this space. This space opens the door for life's most significant moments to unfold.

REFLECTIONS

Turning Pain into Purpose

Giving confirms in me that I have truly been restored. When I was a teacher, one teaching method I used was think-pair-share. When using this tool, you must first learn an idea for yourself, then you find a buddy, and finally, share your new concept. By sharing a new concept, students must find their own words to describe what was just learned. It makes that concept personal. Giving feels like a think-pair-share where I give my hard-earned life lessons. By finding someone experiencing cancer and sharing my heart, I am finding the verbal framework for my own experiences. By sharing my heart, I better understand my own healing. All this is done to encourage someone else, allowing them to learn a new perspective so that they, too, may begin to heal.

Giving provides my pain with a purpose. I often say that for every high, there is a low. In my lowest moments, I felt the need to experience an emotional high. During the weekends before a new chemo session, my family would run away to the mountains or even to Disneyland. I needed those huge boosts to help me walk into the next round of treatments that felt overwhelmingly difficult. Today I live with metastatic cancer. Every day of my life, cancer is there. Running away to the mountains, though amazing, cannot give my daily burdens purpose. Therefore, I choose to live in such a way that I am able to give my disease a daily purpose. A terminal diagnosis requires me to give more back because I perpetually need to experience its meaning. I need to see the good that comes from the burdens I carry.

> **Giving means using what is uniquely you for the sake of someone else.**

> **Serving others without expecting anything in return creates a sense of belonging, confidence, and strength in both individuals.**

PART 2 CONCLUSION:

MILESTONES FOR EMOTIONAL GROWTH

this section began with the acknowledgment that healing and a cure are not the same. Treatments that cure many cancers are significantly easier to walk through than the Seasons of Healing. Treatments come with a checklist, a calendar, a specified number of sessions, and a clear end date. Healing, on the other hand, does not follow a timeline. I cannot say, "After four weeks in the Void you will be free to move forward into a season of Growth. Since we are beginning today, you should be free of this season by Valentine's Day!" This is what we want. We want certainty, a guarantee, an opportunity to ring a bell that tells us everything is okay now, we have done enough. Even if we know the guarantee may not be 100 percent true, we still desire it. It provides us with certainty, something to lean on when our doubts arise. It gives us a sense of accomplishment and a milestone to look to.

While we are moving forward through the grief and trauma we experienced in cancer, emotional healing requires that we create our own milestones. I hope you have been journaling through your healing. A journal can provide you with the very milestones you desire. Through journaling, you provide yourself with an honest look at your own growth. Look back at the beginning of your journals, specifically at the questions you asked and grief you expressed. Are those questions the same ones you are processing today? Is your grief as painful today as it was when you were in the Void? As you look through your journal, highlight some of your thoughts that feel complete in your life now, or some pain that has been resolved. These are your benchmarks! These are milestones demonstrating the healing that has occurred. Don't pass over these private accomplishments, they are significant, a gift you are giving yourself and those you love, and they deserve celebration.

In cancer, we often anxiously anticipate scan results because they provide clear indications of whether or not we are being cured of the disease. In breast cancer, we also track tumor markers, these are the growth impulses in our blood that show what the cancer is trying to do. Tumor markers can indicate if there are cells that will probably become visible cancer in the next six months. When we read through our journals, we can see our mental-growth impulses. These emotional markers are found in our stream of consciousness. When our thoughts are free flowing, with only fear, regret, and pain, it indicates in the next six months we will most likely experience more and more pain points. What is growing in us is fear, hurt, and regret. These will continue to grow unless we take action against them. When we are trying to break cycles of fear by taking every thought captive and our journals are filled with grief and questions that lead us to a deeper understanding, then, in our next six months, there will be room for change. The growth factor in our emotional markers might shift away from growing pain and instead toward a trend of leveling off or moving away from fear. When we find our journals wrestling with hope, looking for the gifts of cancer, acknowledging our pain but not letting that pain define us, then the emotional markers might begin to trend downward, diminishing in the amount of fear and hurt we carry in our free-flowing thoughts. Similar to how a tumor marker might rate cancer's growth in your blood, you can take a look at your own thoughts and rate your levels of hope, your clarity on grief, and your ability to direct your own thoughts.

Though I cannot provide you with a specific timeline for your Seasons of Healing, you can compare your former thoughts with where your thoughts are today. Just as we might compare our scans from six months ago to our scans today, we can compare our journal entries from six months ago to our journal entries now and look for signs of growth.

Our mental health is as important as our physical health and deserves an equal amount of attention and analysis. Just as the body might need to experience short-term pain for the sake of long-term health, our emotional health also needs to fully experience each of the Seasons of Healing in order to truly emerge whole and complete. It is important to recognize, therefore, that self-protection is not the escape or denial of painful situations but the full acknowledgment of them. It is only when we see ourselves in truth that we may find ourselves free of pain. Just as tumors do not shrink without direct intervention, your fear will not shrink unless you take direct action against it. Let me encourage you! Fear can be overcome. Pain and grief will remain a part of life but can be carried with beauty and purpose.

Part 3
Cancering

CANCERING

When life is changed by cancer, it is not for a moment or a season. Cancer shifts our trajectory, altering what we see, feel, expect, and desire. What I never considered before my own cancer experiences was the possibility that this shift could be good. Cancer can be an opportunity because growing, healing, and becoming are a part of cancering.

Before this moment in history, cancer limited life. Today, cancering is a way of life. Cancering means those with a diagnosis live with the presence and impact of this disease for a lifetime. In fact, we are living with cancer more often than we are dying with cancer. We need to stop and mentally acknowledge this shift of expectation.

I have lived with cancer for nine years. I have lived and loved, adventured, and grown. I have designed and developed solutions for how we might better live with cancer, and I have done this all while cancering. Cancering is the future—our future—individually and societally. It is up to us, the first generation of true survivors, to discover and define the possibilities available in the cancering experience—possibilities like compassion, resilience, and community.

Cancering requires us to shift our mindsets. It requires us to expect life, to count on it, plan for it, and keep living it. Cancering requires us to focus on hope and possibilities. We have a lot of baggage to overcome around the word cancer. The cancer of the past has stolen many beautiful people from us. It is important to acknowledge the stories of those who have gone before us and honor the families who ache from those who are absent. However, we must also recognize that as long as we have breath, their stories are not our own. Though the cancer experience is imperfect, we live in a different era. We live in a time of hope.

This moment in the history of cancer provides us the opportunity to live while cancering. How many cancer patients before us were desperate for such a gift, yet how many of us are throwing away this opportunity because we carry the fears of those who went before us? We are the first generation to be offered such a gift, but we cannot receive this gift if we continue to hold on to the past.

The previous sections of this book help us acknowledge and heal from the trauma of cancer. This section points us forward, encouraging us to remain strong while impacted by cancer.

CHAPTER 9

Emotional Health Moving Forward

Keeping our bodies healthy is common knowledge. We are taught basic tools from elementary school and throughout our lives. Doctor's appointments point us toward good choices for ourselves and our families. Public service announcements can be found on city buses and in commercials. If a lifetime of education is not enough, there are dietary guidelines on every packaged food we purchase, helping us to remain informed. All of this work is done to ensure we know that for a healthy body, we need:

1. Rest

2. Water

3. Healthy food

4. Movement

These are the things our bodies need. Whether we have the flu or we scraped our knees while on the monkey bars, these are the ways we find physical healing. We as humans have been living with our bodies and our emotions for the same amount of time, yet there doesn't seem to be an equal amount of effort to educate society on a four-point list for how to maintain emotional health.

Babies are born crying, and even before we care for their physical needs, they are held close and tight and safe. Caring for emotional needs is the very first thing we do for a newborn baby. However, when this baby turns sixteen, emotional health is no longer at the forefront of our minds. Even if we recognize a problem, we are often filled with many more questions than solutions for how to meet these needs. So, when did the shift take place? When did we lose sight of how to care for our emotional wellness and decide our physical wellness was sufficient? At some point, we chose to remain informed on caring for the body but allowed ourselves to become uneducated when it came to caring for emotional health.

In the experience of cancer, there are dozens of people in a patient's life in charge and concerned with maintaining physical health. There are packets for "standard of care" and binders for "just in case." We analyze bloodwork, imaging, and every tiny ache or pain that can be felt. With all this structure and procedure for the body, where do we turn to promote emotional health?

While billions of dollars are spent understanding the unique and mysterious aspects of the body, an equal challenge facing us today is the pursuit of emotional health and healing. In fact, survivors almost unanimously agree that the most challenging aspect of the cancer experience begins when the treatments end. When the physical treatments of cancer end, the emotional work is just beginning. After the trauma of cancer, each of us must find our own way forward. None of us can truly reengage until emotional healing has occurred—but how does that happen?

Our physical health and emotional health are linked in ways that are impossible to calculate, but I suggest we allow our emotional healing to begin by using what we know.

Rest

Suggesting rest to someone who has just been required to stay in bed or on the couch for a year is almost a sucker punch. However, emotional rest doesn't have to be confining.

A cancer diagnosis and treatments require you to live between a foggy, overwhelmed mind full of stress, anxiety, exhaustion, and adrenaline-charged decision-making. There is no rest for the mind during this season. Because of this, it is mandatory that we allow ourselves a season with fewer decisions, less stimulation, and more safety. But this season will not come naturally; it must be created by choice. As your body gains its previous strength, you might be expected to step into a busy schedule with multiple responsibilities. Though your body is regaining strength, your emotional health will not recover at the same rate. When your body was pushed to its physical limits, your mind was pushed as well. However, while you knew to take naps and get extra sleep, you did not have the opportunity to allow your mind and emotions to check out and disassociate themselves from your circumstances. The opportunity for your mind to rest does not begin until the trauma of cancer has ended.

Mental rest is required before your brain and emotions understand that you are no longer in danger. An understanding of safety must be established before your mind can begin to step outside the barricaded fortress it created for your protection.

This is not something that can be rushed. Even though the dust has settled for a week, the mind remains alert, awaiting the next attack. A significant shift must occur in your life before emotional rest can be experienced.

This can be seen in young mothers whose children have cancer. The mother has been juggling decision-making, sleepless nights, and the needs of those she loves. Once treatment is over, she feels exhausted, but she also feels the need to continue to fight for her family. So she will immediately return to work. Work, even on the simplest days, feels overwhelming. All the energy she used to carry her family through the crisis is still bubbling just below the surface. Now, she is a warrior without a war. Without a season of rest, or a time to reset her stress levels, every small issue gets one hundred percent of her emotional energy, focus, and time. She gives one hundred percent of her fighting and surviving energy to a situation that only really needs fifteen percent of her strength. She has lived in and through trauma, and without a time of rest to reset her expectations and care for her emotional health, her mental strength continues to be drained as if the trauma continued.

Have you ever had surgery? After surgery, a doctor says you should take it easy for six weeks. The trauma to your body ended with the last stitch from the doctor, but you need six more weeks to recover. Then two weeks into recovery, you feel much better. You decide to get out of bed, go for a walk, or run a load of laundry. What happens next? The next three days you are in so much pain! The body was not actively hurting, so you pushed it, expecting the same strength and stamina it gave you before the trauma of surgery. Just because the pain goes away, just because the trauma ends, does not mean you are ready to carry the responsibilities that came easily before the trauma—not without a time of rest.

We do this to ourselves emotionally all the time. We wake up and don't feel the pain of the trauma, so we call our boss and say,

"I am ready to come back to work." Three days after returning to work, exhaustion sets in, with no break on the horizon.

To heal emotionally, we need rest. It is very difficult to allow ourselves this rest because we still believe in the value of independent strength. When we cannot point to a physical scar or give any physical indication of our needs, we feel we cannot properly demonstrate or prove the presence of our ongoing recovery. The trauma of cancer has required that others pick up the responsibilities we physically couldn't carry during treatment, so to ask for more support can feel selfish. However, for us to truly overcome cancer, emotional healing must be a priority.

Water

Water washes our bodies clean, on the inside and out. When we are sick, water flushes our system, causing all the toxins to move through us and heal our bodies. When we have a cut, we wash the broken skin with water, eliminating the potential of infection. During our season of emotional healing, we need a similar cleansing to flush out our minds and emotions. The fears we have carried through our trauma are no longer relevant, but if allowed to remain, they will begin to spread, infecting parts of our lives beyond our initial wounding. The emotional toxins we carry through treatment must be released. It is more difficult to flush our emotions because they are invisible to the eye. We cannot look at an emotional wound and see it getting more red and swollen. Also, emotional wounds have a way of becoming familiar. We grow accustomed to carrying them. We may even forget there is another way of being. So, rather than pursuing healing, we adjust our expectations and learn to live with the pain.

When we have an injured leg, we limp. This limp indicates that pain remains, and a wound is present. In a similar way, we must become aware of our emotional habits. We must look honestly at what makes our hearts race and our minds suddenly sound an alert. When do we snap at our kids or loved ones? What is our current emotional lifting capacity? These outbursts of emotional pain, frustration, and stress are reminders that our emotions are still limping along. There are wounds that have not healed. More rest will be required before we can carry a heavy load.

So, how do we begin to rinse these emotional wounds and allow them to heal? As we observe our triggers and the emotional habits in our daily routines, we want to begin renewing our minds. Think of it as emotional rehabilitation. We need to stretch out some sore spots and build up strength that will allow us to reach our emotional-strength goals. We do this by washing away what was useful during trauma and making room for what we need now. To initiate a season of emotional healing, it is important to give the old way of thinking a new place to live. The old thoughts and fears need to get flushed out.

Tools for releasing old emotional patterns of thought are:

- Journaling

- Support Groups

- Cancer Coaching

- Counseling

- Meditation

- Time in Nature

These tools allow you to transfer pent-up emotional energy, thoughts, and feelings into a new format. They allow you to remove thoughts so they don't fill your mind. Creating space begins to reverse the cycle of trauma. These tools nurture you and promote healing. After living through a season of being overburdened, releasing a few disappointments or fears can feel liberating. Don't stop there! You cannot rush this season. The more you wash your thoughts and emotions clean, the less potential remains for long-term negative impact on your emotional health. Remember, healing takes time, but when you rush through the healing process, you will find yourself in pain longer than necessary.

Healthy Food

Once we wash away the emotional habits created during trauma, there is space for something new. We now have the capacity to introduce restorative habits into our daily routines. Through rest and washing out old thought patterns, we make space for our hopes and dreams to emerge. This season of newness shifts our thoughts from what was to what can be. Suddenly, we have the ability to hold fragile dreams. We have new expectations. We discover our values directing us. For these emerging parts of ourselves to grow and thrive, they must be fed healthy emotional food.

Just as our bodies can't simply be given healthy food one day and expect to be healthy for eighty years, our emotional health can't survive on one day of positivity. Our fragile dreams become stronger when our mental habits support them. We must believe in possibilities beyond what are available today. Choosing to feed our thoughts hopeful—even irrationally optimistic—possibilities helps us escape from the limitations fear created. As we come out of a season of physical and emotional limitations, we must retrain our minds. There are no boundaries to what we can imagine. There are no limits to what beautifully hopeful ideas we can create. The only limits that exist are those we allow to remain in our thought patterns. Dreaming of wonderful outcomes is good for our minds, emotions, and bodies! It is healthy to be optimistic. It even heals our bodies when we focus on what is good in life. It is liberating to dwell on the possibilities.

When you begin feeding yourself this healthy emotional food, it might be a struggle at first. Habits must be created to support this way of thinking. It is easy to complain about the weather, traffic, and laundry, but what good can you find even in these mundane circumstances? You must make a choice about how you choose to see the world, and then you must make that choice over and over. Every day will provide you with the opportunity to give up or keep going. Do you feed yourself healthy mental energy or slip into the habit of dwelling on the negative? Every day the "fast food" of emotional habits will be there for you. You can choose doubt, fear, and hesitation. These emotions feel easier to choose when circumstances begin to stack against you. They are often familiar patterns that quickly fill your mind. These habits of "fast food" emotions will never truly allow you to rest. These unhealthy mental habits may allow you to stop choosing a different mental pathway, but they will leave you unsatisfied, uncomfortable, and uneasy.

On the other hand, hope, perseverance, resilience, strength, and integrity are equally available. These healthy emotional habits are not quickly experienced. Each of these emotions requires you to choose them regularly until they become habitual. Like a mother's daily presence in a baby's life blinds her to the way the child is growing, the growth in you might seem absent. While the changes seem imperceptible to you, those surrounding you will witness your growth. Your choices set you on a trajectory, and healthy mental food will lead you closer to the person you want to become.

Movement

Science is showing us more and more that movement is key to a healthy life. Movement impacts every aspect of our bodies. We are designed to move and be in motion, and the more we sit in one place, the less healthy we become. Our mental health is also dependent on movement. Our brains love adventure. They thrive on learning and experiencing new ideas. They want to expand and grow. Our emotions are no different. Our emotions are not meant to get stuck on one way of being. If we are angry and refuse to admit how angry we are, we get angrier. We are not meant to hold onto one way of being, so when we do not let go of an emotion, it grows and grows until we can no longer bear it. If, instead, we admit our anger and talk with the person we are angry with, we begin to feel less anger. Even if the problem does not go away, we have begun to release one state; therefore, we are creating the capacity for another emotional state to emerge.

It is not good for our physical, mental, or emotional health to remain in one emotional state for extended periods of time. Just as we intentionally build time into our lives to walk or work out, we must become aware of the need to move from one emotional state to another. In the case of cancer, fear is a dominant emotion. Fear will remain present in the life of the survivor and co-survivors unless they learn to move past fear once the threat of cancer has passed. Movement from fear to some new emotional state is essential. To remain in a constant state of anger, disappointment, hate, excitement, surprise, or even happiness forever is not an indication of good health. Movement is necessary for life. Establishing the capacity to move from one state to another strengthens our mental and emotional health.

Stepping Forward

As you step beyond cancer, remember to take some time to do a mental and emotional check-up by considering the root of your current thought patterns. When we aerate a lawn, we dig into the hard ground where the grass is trying to grow. We dig small holes, but those small holes promote growth. By aerating the lawn, we allow the roots to receive clean air, water, and nutrients. We break up the hard spaces where roots cannot penetrate. All these things create an opportunity for the roots to go deeper. By digging small holes and creating space in the earth, the roots rejuvenate and create a healthier lawn. Just as grass needs the space aeration provides, our identity needs space to breathe. By setting aside regular times of rest, we create space in our identity and emotions. Through rest, we increase our capacity. As we learned in the Void season, emptiness can uncover what would otherwise be overlooked. To ensure we honor all aspects of our identity, we must create pockets of space or Void areas where our identity can stretch and grow.

Take Action

Set aside time each day without screens or responsibilities. When all external stimuli are removed, where does your mind go? Consider this time as a daily weeding of your thoughts. If an idea is running rampant, pull it out and take a good look at it. Use a journal to write it down. Pull it from the garden of your mind. Write about that thought until you understand why it is there. Follow its roots until you find where it came from. If you fail to track down the root of the thought, it will regenerate because this is the nature of a weed. By pulling out the weeds in your mind, you make space for beauty and joy to grow.

    The tools we learn in this book are fundamental during the emotional healing of cancer, but they are also good tools for life. Cancer is a big trauma that must be dealt with, but there are small griefs that we face every day. When a small grief emerges, it can feel like a tiny thorn in our minds. We try to ignore this mental pain because of how often it occurs. However, if we do not pull it out, that small, thorned weed will take root and grow many friends. What begins as the annoyance of a car cutting you off on your way home will grow into frustration about the price of gas and anger around the slow service at dinner. One small, thorned vine of grief can create a lifetime of pain points.

    Life is difficult, and it causes pain more often than we want to acknowledge. The pursuit of emotional wellness, therefore, is not a one-time event. Healing is an integral part of daily life. As you embrace the seasons, griefs, and joys of life, know emotional wellness is available to you. Seek to renew your mind, take every thought captive, and tend your thoughts so that you may experience the good that surrounds you every day of your life.

REFLECTIONS

Cancering

The first time I lost my hair due to treatments, I only took one picture of myself bald. The idea of cancer and me together was not something I wanted to document. I thought cancer was something I could simply delete from my life's story if I never acknowledged it with a photo. During those first years, I was urgently pushing forward to get to the end of my cancer-treatment timeline. I wanted to get this season behind me so I could continue with my story and pretend as if cancer had never shown up. I have a faith-based foundation shaping how I see the world. However, at my first diagnosis, I kept that purposeful life and my cancer diagnosis separate. Of course, I leaned on my faith for my own strength, but I never considered that this story, this cancering life, could become anything more than a blip in my bigger story. I wanted to escape these circumstances so that I could return to what was really important.

At the time of my second diagnosis, I was required to consider a different possibility. Now there was cancer, and there was me, and somehow the two had to come into alignment. This time, cancer got my attention. Perhaps this was the important story I was meant to tell. Perhaps there was more going on here for me than running away from my difficulties.

> **"Cancering is a mindset that acknowledges how life and cancer connect."**

None of us get to choose the circumstances we will face in life. As for me, I could not escape the fact that cancer would be part of my story. Therefore, I had to decide what kind of story I wanted to tell. What would I do with the life I was given? What would I teach my children about how to face hardships? Where would I point my life when my life's path was suddenly altered? How could I take these weaknesses and allow them to become a strength?

All of us living with cancer must answer these questions. We must find purpose amid pain. Life is full of pain, there is no running away from it. When we stop running away from pain, then we are able to live a deeply meaningful story.

Cancering is a mindset that acknowledges how life and cancer connect. Cancer is not life, and life cannot escape the impact of cancer. As a result, those of us diagnosed with the disease must allow the coexistence of these separate and potentially conflicting trajectories in order to experience an honest and resilient future.

Embracing cancer as part of my story unlocked many of the desires of my heart. I found my voice, people to serve and love, and a mental space that needed someone to bring good news. By choosing to live a cancering life, I was able to transform cancer from my greatest enemy into my strongest ally.

PART 3 CONCLUSION:
THE 30,000-FOOT VIEW

a 30,000-foot view of the world smooths out the ups and downs of mountains and valleys. You cannot observe the thorns on the roses or the difficult and broken road that one must travel from point A to point B because this perspective tells a different story. It is the big picture, a beautiful expanse that stretches out in every direction. A 30,000-foot view of life widens our experience of a moment. Rather than focusing on the difficult details of the day, we are reminded of how our lives are integrated into so many other lives. How our healing can inspire healing in those around us in ways we may never fully understand. We are reminded of how we are established in a particular place and time. We are reminded that the fabric of our lives is woven together with our histories, our geographic locations, our decisions, and our hopes. We are bigger than this moment or these struggles. We are releasing ripples into our communities. We are reshaping the future of our family history. We are breaking off the mistakes of our parents and their parents and becoming something altogether new. A 30,000-foot view of life helps us remember why we work to heal. It isn't simply for today, it is for tomorrow's tomorrow, for our children's children. The impact we have in this space and time will shape the lives of countless generations, none of which we can see from this singular moment.

Cancering is about minimizing the pain in our own lives, but, from a bigger perspective, it is also about minimizing pain and brokenness in the generations that follow us. We can only pass down what we have. If we have a life of fear and pain, we will give that to our children, and they will give it to theirs. If we pursue restorative healing, we will provide our children with the tools to pursue healing in their lives as well. It is our pursuits and not our accomplishments that will inspire our children. We are not required to achieve perfection or even eliminate fear or pain completely. It is the pursuit of healing that matters. It is that we desire for ourselves and our families something different, a life of hopeful adventures. Our children will not fault us for lacking all the answers, they will only carry regret if we never search for any answers at all.

This book is as much for the next generation as it is for those living with cancer today. I know cancer in future generations will be different, but their emotional burdens will remain the same unless we begin to change how cancer impacts us today.

EPILOGUE

When I defined the Void season, I talked of holding grief in one hand and hope in the other. In that season, we must learn to be at peace with both the changing expectations of the past and the unknowable future. The cancering life requires us to continue in this stance, living with both hands open. Hope and grief are perpetually present, beauty and scars coexist, joy and pain intermingle, love and loss are bound together as one. These tools for emotional restoration are given to you so that you might live a resilient life. Resilient, because life is not easy. This book is not written to make an argument for an easy, happy, nice life. It is written that you might have tools when life is overwhelming, hope when scans are not good, and love even when you feel alone. This book is a tool kit for the hard times, because difficult is not the same as bad. Yes, we must struggle, but those struggles are able to make us stronger, truer, and more resilient every time.

The cancering life is abundant with gifts that have the ability to give us strength while carrying the burdens of cancer. However, sometimes these gifts are difficult to receive. I acknowledge there are lessons in this book that will feel very difficult to receive. I ask that you do not dismiss these lessons right away. Let them sit with you for a while. Come back to them in six months and then in a year. As you grow and heal, you might find the lessons become easier to receive.

I told you from the beginning, I am not an expert. I am a patient, survivor, thriver, mother, and wife chasing a vision of what might be. I am hoping that by walking out this possibility I am able to create a path for others to follow me. Mental well-being is obtainable in and through cancer. Emotional restoration is a possibility for all of us. The potential for post-traumatic growth is within us if we only have the tools to allow it to emerge. This is my hope and expectation for all of us. I believe the future of cancer will be different when we find the tools for emotional restoration. May this book be one of the tools you reach for when the pain points emerge again.

I know how hard this path is, I know it is exhausting, I know it is heartbreaking. I also know that if we keep walking, keep living, and keep hoping, we will find ourselves in places we have only imagined. The thrill of walking out a new path is not knowing what is around the next bend. It is this mystery in life, this adventure of the unknown, that piques our senses and calls us forward. Life is an adventure if and only if we are expecting to find good things at the end of the trail. So when you face a season that beats down on you, keep walking, just around the turn I expect you will find a beautiful spring-fed pool of water that will give you rest.

About the Author

Lauren Huffmaster is a metastatic breast cancer survivor currently residing in the San Francisco Bay Area. Since her diagnosis in 2015, she has embarked on a transformative journey, emerging as a speaker, a certified Cancer Journey Coach, the founder of Adventure Therapy Foundation, and the host of the podcast *Adventures with Scars*.

Drawing from her own experiences with cancer, Lauren possesses a unique perspective and an unwavering commitment to reshaping the cancer narrative. Her mission is to redefine cancer survivorship and inspire others to embrace hope and resilience on their personal journeys.

To book Lauren as your next inspirational speaker or podcast guest, please contact her at lauren@adventurefound.org.

Who We Are:
While many organizations concentrate on the physical challenges of cancer, Adventure Therapy Foundation was created specifically to help heal the equally devastating emotional side effects of the disease.

Mission:
The Adventure Therapy Foundation is a nonprofit organization committed to acknowledging and defining the emotional side effects of cancer, thereby facilitating a more comprehensive and genuine healing process for those impacted by cancer.

What We Do: No one tells you about the emotional side effects of cancer. We do. We not only talk about them, but we also work to break the destructive cycles they create. We do this by providing educational and experiential programs that minimize cancer's impact.

For more information or to make a charitable donation visit:
AdventureFound.org
info@adventurefound.org
EIN: #61-1896557

Made in the USA
Middletown, DE
16 May 2025

75579656R00116